SPIRITUALITY UNVEILED

SPIRITUALITY UNVEILED

AWAKENING TO CREATIVE LIFE

Santoshan
(Stephen Wollaston)

FOREWORD BY IAN MOWLL

BOOKS

Winchester, UK
Washington, USA

First published by O-Books, 2011
O Books is an imprint of John Hunt Publishing Ltd.,
The Bothy, Deershot Lodge, Park Lane, Ropley,
Hants, SO24 0BE, UK
office1@o-books.net
www.o-books.com

For distributor details and how to order
please visit the 'Ordering' section on our website.

Text copyright: Santoshan (Stephen Wollaston) 2010

ISBN: 978 1 84694 509 0

A CIP catalogue record for this book is available from the British Library.

Design: Santoshan (Stephen Wollaston).
Back cover photograph: Tony Russell.
Page twelve painting: Nika Dunnwald (www.woodvibrations.de).

'Twelve Principles of Creation Spirituality' quoted with permission from
Originally Blessed, edited by Matthew Henry,
published by Creation Spirituality Communities.

Printed in the UK by CPI Antony Rowe.
Printed in the USA by Offset Paperback Mfrs, Inc.

O Books operates a distinctive and ethical publishing philosophy in all areas
of its business, from its global network of authors to production and
worldwide distribution.

This book is dedicated to the spiritual heroes who have sought to cross all boundaries and establish peace in the world, and have encouraged a more caring attitude towards Mother Earth and all life upon her, and to those who have joined them in their quest and put their wisdom into practice.

*The first peace, which is the most important, is that which comes
within the souls of people when they realize their relationship,
their oneness with the universe and all its powers, and when they
realize that at the centre of the universe dwells the Great Spirit
and that this centre is really everywhere, it is within each of us.*
– BLACK ELK

*[We] must decide to live with a sense of universal responsibility,
identifying ourselves with the whole Earth community as well
as our local communities. We are at once citizens of different
nations and of one world in which the local and global are linked.
Everyone shares responsibility for the present and future
well-being of the human family and the larger living world.
The spirit of human solidarity and kinship with all life is
strengthened when we live with reverence for the mystery of
being, gratitude for the gift of life, and humility regarding the
human place in nature.*
– EARTH CHARTER, PREAMBLE, PARAGRAPH 5

CONTENTS

ACKNOWLEDGEMENTS

I wish to thank John Chapman, a member of Thich Nhat Hanh's Order of Interbeing (Tiep Hien), for generously assisting with the proof reading and making constructive comments, and June Raymond, a sister of Notre Dame, for having a sharp eye for noticing typing errors. But it goes without saying that any mistakes that might remain, are entirely my own.

I also wish to give a special thanks to Matthew Henry for giving permission to quote Twelve Principles of Creation Spirituality in one of the Appendices, the harpist and Tibetan Buddhist, Nika Dunnwald, for allowing me to use one her beautiful paintings for the inside of this book, and Ian Mowll, the coordinator of GreenSpirit, for kindly writing the Foreword and sharing his passion for what he describes as *community storytelling*, which profoundly draws attention to the deeper dimensions of spirituality.

Finally, a big thanks goes to John, Trevor, Maria and Stuart at O Books for their patience and help in leading me through their production process.

Painting by Nika Dunnwald

FOREWORD
BY IAN MOWLL

We live in times of great change. Perhaps the greatest changes in all of human history are happening now within our current age. We can travel halfway around the world in a single day. We can see into space and understand the workings of the smallest atom. Our Earth's environment is changing before our eyes, and our relationships and communities are both transforming in ways that past generations could not have possibly imagined.

Some of these changes are for the better, whereas some are for the worse. Like other forward looking thinkers, I believe that contemporary spirituality needs to resonate with our changing world, to provide us with inspiration that can refresh our relationships with our friends, our community and with the Earth.

I should mention at this stage that I have a passion for making a point by using the ancient method of telling a story, so if you, the reader, will excuse me for a few pages, I would like to tell you about a relative of mine.

Some years ago I was at a family party, at which I was told my second cousin, Andrew Wiles from Princeton University, was also present. Various relatives were keen to tell me he was a mathematician, researching 'number'. I thought about speaking to him, but he seemed so quiet and with so little to say that it did not seem worth my while. So I passed on this opportunity and spoke to other relatives instead.

A few days later I was working in New York and there on a desk in front of me was a picture of Andrew! He was on the front page of the New York Times and was mentioned in an article titled, *At Last, Shout of 'Eureka!' in Age-Old Math Mystery*. He had achieved a major breakthrough in mathematics it seemed, something that mathematicians had devoted their whole careers to try and solve for numerous centuries. He had in fact accomplished what was thought to be impossible by some.

The article went on to mention how Andrew had read a book about the problem of *Fermat's Last Theorem* at the age of 10, and how he had made it his dream to solve it. Whenever he had the opportunity to work on it, he seized the chance with both hands. He was also asked in the article about his method of research and replied that, "You enter the first room of the mansion and it's completely dark. You stumble around bumping into the furniture but gradually you learn where each piece of furniture is. Finally, after six months or so, you find the light switch, you turn it on, and suddenly it's all illuminated. You can see exactly where you were."

Then in 1993, after 7 years of working on the problem, he thought he had solved it, and so, at a lecture at Cambridge University, he announced his success. This was in fact the day after I saw him at the family party. The news quickly spread around the world trumpeting his achievement.

Now he has become Sir Andrew Wiles and has numerous prestigious awards in Mathematics and is quite likely to go down as one of the most famous mathematicians of all time. And to think that I thought he was too boring to speak to!

I do not write about Andrew specifically about his talent of course, because I believe that everybody is special in their own way, but because it shows that if I had taken the time to dig beneath the surface, to see more than a shy, retiring academic, I would have found an inspirational story of struggle, ability and conquest. And so, to get to the point of why I am telling you this, is that this is sometimes how we can view the world. We might look upon the surface of everyday life and it may seem to us as being mundane or commonplace. Everyday familiarity can bring us down into a passionless treading of water that leads nowhere. But if, like Andrew, we have the courage to explore and sometimes stumble around in the dark until we find a light switch, we will begin to find new, unexpected and hidden truths.

This is why this book is so important. Stephen has written this book with both breadth and insight, drawing from numerous sources, and has succeeded in shining a steady and clear beacon to help illuminate our understanding. So, with the help of this book, it is time for us to stop bumping around in the dark and to turn the light switch on – to glimpse into some of life's deepest depths and hidden treasurers, and in so doing, replenish our relationships with our human community, with all life and the precious Earth on which we live. I invite you to read on...

PREFACE

This book is a collection of shared thoughts and teachings, which are about the varieties of creative forces within us and around us. It is about creative development as a continual active path. If followed with sincerity and openness, these teachings will lead you, just as they have me, through many landscapes – through times of joy and sadness, through times of light and darkness – and will awaken you to see everything as part of the journey to healthy growth.

The following pages highlight wisdom that both I and many others who have been strongly drawn to a creative, and creation centred, spirituality have found deeply beneficial in their spiritual lives. For our current age calls us all to embrace an inclusive, universal and creative spirituality; one that encompasses living the whole of our life as skilfully, peacefully and lovingly as possible, and manifesting qualities that lead to recognizing the profound unity we share with all people and Nature and the indispensable responsibilities this brings. Ultimately, although we are travelling through a multiple of spheres – such as a spirit world, an ecological world and a psychological world – it is a single integration that seeks interaction with the all-ness of healthy and abundant living.

The beauty of our physical Earth is a profound expression of the spirit in matter. When we include the natural world in our unfoldment, we open to an ancient path that has been recognized by many great traditions – one that is *life affirming*. Through deep contact with the essentials of spiritual growth, we awaken to cosmic realms of spirituality, which are by their very nature, universally all-inclusive and creative.

Traditional wisdom that links with this path can be found in Yogic teachings, particularly Kashmir Shaivism, about *all* the chakras and *shakti* energy (an active and creative and cosmic power embedded within Nature and the workings of the universe) and in the insights of some of the Christian mystics, with aspects of Sufi, Buddhist, Daoist, Ancient Celtic, Australian Aboriginal, Native American, Hasidic Jewish, Neo-Pagan and African Bush People's spirituality. It is a path as old as creation itself, because of its connections with the creative force and mind that has pervaded the universe since its birth.

The very first flaring forth of creation, Ellen Bernstein tells us in *The Green Bible*, was seen by early rabbis as the first revelation of God in the universe. Before any God of scripture or God of humans, there has been a God of Nature. For God has been communing with Nature for longer than any human centred spiritual or religious tradition. If the entire Earth's history was compared to a calendar year, only the last few seconds would in fact consist of human activity.

In recent years Matthew Fox has popularly highlighted teachings about *original blessing*, which has strong roots in many traditions that affirm our original goodness – the blessing of life and the spiritual gifts we all possess and have the potential for. As far back as Genesis we find teachings that remind us that, "God saw all that he made and it was very good." (1:31). Awakening to our original goodness comes about through the realisation that goodness and divinity are not separate from us, but are integral parts of our being.

In the process of creative unfoldment, nothing is seen in isolation, but continually worked with and through to achieve a harmonious synthesis of the whole of who and what we are – including the realisation that we are ultimately, "spiritual beings having a human experience", as Teilhard de Chardin reminded us – and our relationship with all. In the process of development, all areas of life will influence us in an infinite variety of ways and make the paths we individually tread unique.

The following pages cover numerous practices and teachings found in a vast variety of wisdom traditions and inspiring contemporary perspectives that connect with this approach and its implications for living. It is a path on which there are many awakenings along the way. If someone were to ask what this involves, it can be summarised in the following ways:

1. The unity and creativity of the divine in the universe.

2. The equality of all species.

3. The omnipresence of a spiritual dimension in everyday life.

4. The continuous evolvement of life and consciousness.

5. Collective, individual, social and global responsibility.

6. The effects of positive and negative actions.

7. Harmonious living with Earth's biodiversity.[1]

When we look into the heart of spirituality, it becomes clear that it encompasses opening to and working with infinite degrees of experience that profoundly link with these areas, where different levels of action are required. While *having responsibility* and *positive actions* connect with realms of ethical choices, *harmonious living with our Earth* is something that has to flow spontaneously and naturally from us, as a response to recognizing our interdependence with Nature. *Unity* and an *omnipresent spiritual dimension* underlay spheres of oneness and non-separateness that many of the world's great spiritual teachers have seen as being the ultimate ground of all life and activity.

1. As a general preference, the word 'Earth' has been written without 'the' in this book – as in 'the Earth' – in order to refer to the name of our home planet in the same manner as other planets, and as more of a living organism and less as an object.

INTRODUCTION

There is a communion with God,
and a communion with earth,
and a communion with God through earth.
— Pierre Teilhard de Chardin

As splendid and awe inspiring as some of the world's great cathedrals, mosques and temples are, they were often built with the aim of transporting people to a different place – to a world beyond the physical world. There is nothing wrong with this. The buildings are celebrations of the spirit, creative abilities, profound teachings and visionary ideas. Nonetheless, they can be seen to miss an essential element of spirituality that is not only about a vertical transcendence to sacred and divine realms, but also a horizontal embracing of the divine in all.

Early indigenous cultures, such as the Native Americans and Australian Aborigines, all had strong roots in Nature based forms of spirituality, and many of them have kept this element as a central part of their beliefs and practices. For them, the divine is often experienced and revered as an all-pervading sacred mystery and power, continually revealing itself and present in the seasons and other workings of Nature (I use the word *sacred* here in reference to the more eastern understanding of the divine/God in all things and the precious gift of life itself). Their understanding of life often helps them to live at one with and respect the natural world without damaging its delicate balance.

Native American culture, along with other indigenous traditions, call our universe's Creator, *the Great Spirit*. Daoist spirituality, which has roots in shamanistic practices and a belief in an interactive world of departed ancestors and spirits, teaches about *the all-pervading Dao*, which can be seen as an ever-present important energy that is particularly found in the workings of the natural world. An understanding of God in its universal form is embedded in Christian teachings about the Cosmic Christ, in the writings and poetry of Christian mystics, such as Hildegard of Bingen and Francis of Assisi, and in Paul's letter to the Romans, where he declares that God's invisible qualities, eternal power and divine nature can be clearly seen in the things that have been made (1:20). For spirituality is not an escape to somewhere else, but in the daily play of bountiful life dwelling within and around us, and in our interactions with other people and species.

As with all great teachings, there is a need to reflect on what they imply in order to discover their deeper meaning. Although we might have to work hard to find mention of the divinity of Nature in the four canonical Gospels, former Archbishop William Temple noticed how Jesus saw a close relationship between God and the natural world:

Jesus taught men to see the operation of God in the regular and the normal – in the rising of the sun and the falling of the rain and the growth of the plants.

This cosmic and Nature based realm of spirituality is also found in sacred Hindu images of dancing Shiva (Shiva-Nataraj), where he is depicted dancing in the heart of all creation. The holy book of the Sikh tradition, the Guru Granth Sahib, tells us to, "Rejoice in the Lord who dwells in nature." Although various traditions and teachings have been reminding us about cosmic and omnipresence spheres of divinity for hundreds of years, it is only recently that we have come to possess clear scientific evidence and knowledge about life's incredible journey, from its spectacular start to our current point in the universe's history.

In the past, it seems that practically all cultures had their creation stories, which gave meaning, purpose and direction to people's lives, and invariably united communities in shared beliefs. Early indigenous people grasped their deep relationship with an interrelated spirit world by drawing upon their ancient stories, symbolism and metaphors that had profound life affirming meaning and helped them to relate to the natural world and cosmos. Their everyday lives and beliefs were intimately intertwined with the universe and the world of Nature, which were often celebrated in shared rituals and gave their communities spiritual purpose. Although occasionally this was sadly not always extended outside of their supportive communities. A down side to small tribal communities is that a mentality of *us* and *them* can still persist.

Yet without their stories and shared rituals they would not have known who they were or how to interact with the world around them, as the stories gave them identity and helped them to understand where they stood in the greater scheme of things. The lay monk Wayne Teasdale also reminded of this:

> *Native Americans know that all beings are part of the web of life, and we have responsibilities to this great web of interconnection. Native cultures are keenly aware that nature, the earth, the Great Spirit, and the spirit guides have taught them everything they know. It is all a gift from the divine realm through the mediation of these more familiar spirit guides who inhabit all worlds.*

Yet in the light of contemporary science, many of the ancient stories of indigenous cultures have lost much of their power and relevance to the age in which we now live. Our understanding of how stars, galaxies and organic life came into being no longer matches a lot of their contents, though some writers, such as Ellen Berstein, have revisited the Bible's account of creation and have beautifully highlighted its deep ecological message. But for many, these early accounts of creation are no longer a part of their lives. Partly because of this, as well as mass urbanisation, many of us have lost our connection with Earth and the sacred element of life that early indigenous cultures recognized. Contemporary materialistic life has drawn many away from having an intimate relationship with a divinity and spirit world that is present in both the seen and unseen. Having no shared story at all that we truly treasure has been seen by authors and teachers, such as the late modern day prophet of eco-spirituality Thomas Berry (who referred to himself as a geologian, rather than a theologian), as a contributory factor to why many are finding postmodern life to be so empty, meaningless and lacking spiritual direction. A contemporary teaching has been recognized by teachers such as Berry to be needed for humankind to reconnect with its roots and the age old quest for discovering the purpose of life, why we are here, where we are going and our unique place in a spiritual universe.

But unlike ancient creation myths – as Joel Primack and Nancy Ellen Abrams point out in their excellent book *View from the Centre of the Universe* – this has to be a contemporary factual and flexible account that is not bound to just one tradition. It needs to be a part of an ongoing search for truth, based on new insights and discoveries, which will help us to build harmonious communities where *everyone* feels valued and able to use their abilities, and express their creativity in fertile and supportive environments.

On the whole, contemporary western societies have lost something essential by no longer possessing shared beliefs and teachings, and not realising that they can often help us to awaken to a significant relationship with Earth. When we have nothing to bring us together and find a deep sense of belonging, we often clog-up our lives with material products we do not necessarily need and cannot supply us with lasting happiness. We often immerse ourselves in pursuits that lead us away from connecting healthily with others, and finding an authentic spirituality that profoundly enriches us.

A simple remedy is to reconnect with the creative and dynamic universe in which we live – to rediscover our roots and our ultimate spiritual heritage. Rabbi Michael Lerner writes about this in *Spirit Matters*:

We are the heirs of the long evolution of Spirit. Each of us is the latest unfolding of the event of Creation. Our bodies are composed of the material that was shaped in the Big Bang. And, so, too, our spirit. The loving goodness of the universe breathes us and breathes through us, giving us life and consciousness, and the capacity to recognize and love others.

In a talk given at a seminar on meditation, celebrating the life and teachings of John Main, the Benedictine monk, Father Laurence Freeman, mentioned how he ran Back to Basics courses for troubled teenagers suffering from depression and low self-esteem, where they would spend time in the countryside learning how to do without many of the things they had come to see as so important in their lives, such as fashion items, mobile phones and other electrical and often expensive, yet ultimately expendable, gadgets. He mentioned how they would often complain at first, but by the end of the course they found a different set of values that gave them a deeper and more lasting sense of happiness, as well as confidence in themselves. They found themselves becoming more contented when their lives were simplified and began to appreciate the true beauty of Nature and being able to relate authentically to others on less superficial levels.

DEEPER
CONNECTIONS

CHAPTER
ONE

*Everything in the universe is energy or a manifestation
of energy, and the purpose of spiritual work is to become
one with that flow of higher creative energy coming
from God through the cosmos.*

— SWAMI RUDRANANDA

When we look deeply into ourselves, we discover
an intuitive knowledge of the profound connections
we share with the creativity of Earth, God, Nature and the
cosmos that mystics, such as the *bhakti*/devotional poet-saint
Kabir profoundly reminded us about: "God is in creation and
creation is in God. God fills all spaces with His presence."

This essential cosmic and Nature based spirituality has
been largely forgotten in the search for human progress.
People can also feel threatened when we take this route, as
it means placing our true growth in our own hands and not
in the direction of others who may have issues of power to
exert. There have been times in the history of the Christian
Church where it has even attempted to suppress it, for fear
of it affecting the Church's influence on society and because
of its teachings about original sin and the fall of humankind

having associations with Nature. Yet original sin is a relatively late doctrine that was not accepted until the 5th century CE, after being introduced by St. Augustine of Hippo (354-430 CE). Instead of our original nature being seen as good and as a blessing, and life, creativity and creation as divine gifts from God, the natural world was separated from the spirit.

Thankfully, cosmic and Nature centred spiritualities were never completely forgotten – sometimes they lasted as undercurrents in various cultures, as seen in the myth of the Green Man in the British Isles and various Wiccan practices – and are essential ingredients in many important teachings about our interactive relationship with the world and the universe. Now, more than ever before, there is a growing and desperate need to reclaim our kinship with Earth, and cosmic and physical dimensions of spirituality that were once so central to human culture.

Cosmic and Nature based realms of spirituality
Deep within the majority of children and adults there is a natural sense of awe and wonder experienced when they look up at the multitude of stars that can be seen at night, or contemplate the rich beauty of our Earth and its colossal array of plants, flowers, trees, insects, animals and birds. At weekends and on holidays we often feel impelled to escape our brick and concrete buildings to find time to rediscover this natural element of spirituality – to be rejuvenated and spontaneously healed whilst being amongst the dazzling colours and aromatic smells of diverse plants and the amazing wildlife of the countryside, or by contemplating breathtaking

rolling hills, majestic mountain ranges, dappled textures of sunlight penetrating lush forests, or the crashing and rolling waves of a roaring sea. Ellen Bernstein points out how our experience of such things can lead to important changes in our spiritual selves:

> *The experience of creation's beauty can engage us more deeply in the world ...*
>
> *Seeing the whole world as beautiful requires a change in us. We must become open and vulnerable if we are to experience the fullness of beauty. Beauty ... bids us to give up our self-centredness and teaches us to care.*

People suffering from severe depression have been known to recover spontaneously when rediscovering a deep connection with Nature. When a dolphin lost its way and unfortunately swam up the River Thames in London, hundreds of people were reported to have flocked to see it each day and became concerned about its welfare. Children with autism have become less traumatised when they have been taken horse riding. There is something in Nature's wildness that draws us out of ourselves. When people came face to face with an incredibly rare white stag in the Cornish countryside a few years back, they often described how the experience was unforgettable and profoundly mystical. Tragically, the obsession some humans have for blood sports, brought a premature end to this amazing animal's life.

Something inexplicable happens to us when we are in deep contact with Nature, and silently take in and absorb its wondrous workings. Even much of our basic and everyday routines are placed around the patterns of the solar system. We generally prefer to sleep at night and plan our holidays when the seasons are at their most favourable. One of the previous Deans of Westminster, Michael Mayne, pointed out that,

There is about us, if only we have eyes to see, a creation of such spectacular profusion, spendthrift richness, and absurd detail, as to make us catch our breath in astonished wonder.

The non-separateness of the sacred

When we acknowledge deeper dimensions of Nature, we touch realms of experience that have been realised by many of the world's great shamans, seers, mystics and prophets. We in fact become shamans, seers, mystics and prophets ourselves when we realise that God is in all, and how all things are ultimately in God. We recognize the intrinsic spark of divinity and divine consciousness that unites us. We awaken to the non-separateness of the spirit and discover that physical life is wondrously embedded in divine existence. This boundless aspect of being is always there inviting us and is an expression of supreme creativity that intimately connects us with the powers of the universe, which can be manifested in each moment and called upon to benefit the world in which we live. Spirituality is in many ways about being awake to this potential, and the abilities and possibilities that are available to us at all times, which can lead us to be spontaneously creative and to participate skilfully in life as it unfolds.

Although our physical senses create the perception of being separate, we need to realise that what we have fed into our unconscious, affects our conscious awareness of life. We invariably create a reality that leads us away from recognizing our true selves. Even so, there are times in which we know instinctively when we touch authentic qualities of our being, such as moments when we are alone in Nature, are simply there for others when they are in need, and that unwholesome behaviour, such as aggression, abuse and egocentricity, are not natural facets of our true selves.

No boundaries

It is because of our past conditioning that we see ourselves as physically separate from other life, which then causes egocentric actions. Our senses create the appearance of being singular and distinctly set apart from other people and objects and life around us and in the universe. Yet not only do the Buddha's and many of the world's great mystical teachings tell us that this is a wrong perception, but quantum physics has also discovered this to be true. On a sub-atomic level there is no clear boundary between different forms of life, objects and phenomenon. Physicists call this interconnectedness *entanglement*. The whole universe is a part of our being and we are a part of the whole universe. The highly respected teacher of and writer on Yogic and ancient Vedic wisdom, David Frawley, tells us that,

We are Nature and all of Nature moves through us. We cannot be apart even if we try. We overflow into all Being, which

ever arises within us through our very blood and breath. Our true civilization is that of the cosmos, not that of one nation or one species only. Our current alienation from the conscious universe is a dangerous detour from our real evolutionary path, which we must not let continue.

We must once again embrace nature within and around us, not merely as body but also as spirit.

The fascinating research of the Cambridge biologist Rupert Sheldrake into morphogenic fields and resonance, has also shown an interconnected psychic element in Nature. Some Yogic teachings tell us that everything, including the creative sound of *Om,* emerged from a cosmic form of *bindu* – a source point and centre of energy (comparable perhaps with the Big Bang Theory). It is said that this also manifests individually within us. From *bindu* all the chakras are said to emerge with their own energy centres and associated elements, forming and culminating in the creation of individualised existence and making our psychic being a microcosm of macrocosmic creative forces at work in the universe.

For the great Hindu philosopher and sage, Ramanaja, the whole world was seen as Vishnu's/God's body. "All are but parts of one stupendous whole, Whose body nature is, and God the soul", Alexander Pope succinctly and poetically wrote.

IN THE BEGINNING
AND IN EVERY
MOMENT

CHAPTER
TWO

*An immersion into the deep creative powers of
the universe is the most direct contact a human can
have of the divine.*

– THOMAS BERRY

Whether we possess scientific, spiritual or religious belief, we will believe that life and the universe hold many waiting to be discovered wonders – that beyond the surface appearance of separate physical forms there are other realities at play within the cosmos. We in fact live in a universe of interconnected pure energy and consciousness that is forever in the act of changing and creating. Creation is ongoing, not a single event. Writing from a Sufi perspective, one of the world's leading experts on Islamic thought and spirituality, Seyyed Hossein Nasr, points out that,

> *The Sufis also speak of creation not only as an act in the past but also as a continual process. This is what is called the renewal of creation at every instant.*

For the spiritually and religiously minded, the ultimate

oneness and ground of being is described in numerous ways, such as the Dao, Spirit, Brahman, Allah, God, Yahweh, or eternal Buddha Nature. In many of the world's great spiritual traditions, this reality is seen as having feminine qualities: as being creative, life-giving, nurturing, inclusive, all-embracing and compassionate. "Be compassionate as your Creator in heaven is compassionate", Jesus taught in Luke's Gospel (6:36). In the Yogic tradition – particularly in Tantra Yoga – which is not a religion, but various paths of spiritual practice that include devotion (bhakti yoga), good works (karma yoga) and discerning wisdom (jnana yoga), the power that brings all things into being is looked upon as *shakti*: the all-pervading active and creative divine Mother energy, which interacts with *prakrti*/Nature. In Neo-Pagan and Wiccan traditions, this power is also described as the divine feminine; for God is as much Mother as Father (lovingly compassionate and wise, immanent and transcendent).

Yet for the sceptically minded, the entire universe came into being through a haphazard accident, and all life on our beautiful blue and white marbled planet is seen as the workings of a random force pushing it forward with no specific goal in mind. This is by no means a new idea. Ever since humans started to contemplate the beginning of the cosmos and life on Earth, they have wondered whether or not there is a creative mind animating it, which is responsible for creating life and, if so, whether life and the universe have a spiritual purpose.

It may appear like a difference between being scientifically and rationally minded, or spiritual and religious in our outlook.

Although traditionally, science has been more concerned with the workings of the cosmos, while spiritual and religious seekers have often searched for meaning behind it, there are millions who are drawn to contemplating spiritual and religious matters who are deeply rational and hold contemporary scientific beliefs that are central to their understanding of life. There are and have been many scientists who are and were religious. Personally I find it irrational to put our experiences of life aside and believe that the harmony, balance, complexity and patterns that can be observed inter-playing in Nature's and the universe's workings as mere coincidences.

Interestingly, the Indian philosopher, Mahendra Nath Sarkar, pointed out as far back as 1943 that, "Science today is passing gradually into a mysterious universe by leaving off the rigid determinism of surface-life and discovering the spontaneity of life." Contemporary physicists and scientific philosophers, such as Joel Primack and Nancy Ellen Abrams, are indeed discovering that humans hold a special place in a living universe that is not without significance (as seen in their book *The View from the Centre of the Universe*).

There is clearly a uniqueness to our being and the diverse forms of life that live and have lived on Earth, and a wondrous sacredness in the astounding continuous unfolding of the universe. To live is a blessing and the birth of any creature, planet or solar system is a miraculous event that must surely never be taken for granted. When we truly cherish the amazing workings of all things, we find ourselves starting to care more deeply about Mother Earth and every creature, activity and species upon her, and protecting life's essential biodiversity, natural balance and harmony.

Essential for seekers drawn to creative forms of growth, such as Creation Centred Spirituality, GreenSpirit (which is a UK based network of CCS) and Deep Ecology, is an acceptance of contemporary scientific discoveries – including insights about human addictions that ecopsychology reveals.

Creation Spirituality embraces an understanding of the divine as continually creating and being present within all things. This contrasts sharply with rigid fundamentalist ideas of creation, which promote a *literal* belief in a series of events happening within a relatively not too distant past, starting creation and completing it in seven days. There is of course no scientific evidence for this, whereas creation, as we know and can see with our own eyes, is still happening today. A recent discovery has been that even rocks themselves evolve. In the history of our planet, hundreds of new minerals have formed that did not exist before. Interestingly, some believe that a theory of evolution would leave no room for a Creator, but what it actually has no space for, is a fundamentalist perspective of life.

An expanding spiritual universe

Contemporary science supplies us with a clear picture about our living and evolving universe. Everything burst forth from a single dynamic quantum event 13.7 billion years ago and possessed a spiritual dimension from the point it came into being. All energy and everything within the universe, owes its origins and existence to this miraculous initial burst of energy, including not only organic life, but also the birth of space, gravity, matter and what scientist sometimes refer to as *space-time continuum* (the concept of time as we normally think of it, being a human construct).

It is now recognized that conditions for our universe to survive its spectacular birth had to be accurate to the smallest fraction of a second. If the rate of spacial unfoldment or the power of gravity had fluctuated too much one way or the other, the whole thing would have either exploded or collapsed, and would never have come to create ideal conditions for organic life to take shape. All things that we witness around us today, owe their origins to this major event. The physicist Brian Swimme along with Thomas Berry, elegantly remind us of this in their truly wonderful book, *The Universe Story*:

> *The vitality of a dolphin as it squiggles high in the summer sun, then, is directly dependent upon the elegance of the dynamics at the beginning of time. We cannot regard the dolphin and the first Flaring Forth [of the universe] as entirely separate events. The universe is a coherent whole, a seamless multi-levelled creative event.*

God in all things

Through deeply reflecting on the incredible evolvement of life, two influential spiritual giants of the 20th century – the French priest, mystic and palaeontologist, Teilhard de Chardin, and the Indian sage and systemiser of modern Integral Yoga, Sri Aurobindo – were led to recognize the existence of a creative divine mind and intelligence that is ever-present and continually expressing itself in and through its workings, and seeking to lead all life to a profound point of spiritual unity (a point where the universal cosmic spirit recognizes itself in all). Teilhard de Chardin called this mystical event the *omega point*. Sri Aurobindo described it as the *supermind*, which he saw as a supreme superconscious phenomenon and projection of the divine, acting in and supporting the universe.

Both were among the first to contemplate humankind's unique place in the cosmos from contemporary scientific perspectives. Both taught about divine consciousness penetrating creation and integrating all in a final stage of unity and how at every stage as lower levels of consciousness are transcended, they are also integrated into higher ones – an evolving process of including and transcending, which the popular integral philosopher Ken Wilber also highlights in his writings. Importantly for Sri Aurobindo, this also meant an embodiment of new states of awareness. For Teilhard de Chardin evolution underlies everything from the simplest sub-atomic particle to the most complex formations of life. Yet the first stage is primarily about *involution* in order for divine consciousness to begin its creative adventure.

But no matter what names or ideas we wish to associate with this creative force, or whether we wish to see it as either masculine or feminine, it is clear that this omnipresent sea of activity at work in our universe is eternally giving life to new forms. The realisation of this deeper mystery has been recognized by numerous seers throughout the ages, who also discovered that we are intrinsically interconnected with, and are unique expressions of, this dynamic power that unites and works through all.

Although no two humans, snowflakes or blades of grass are identical, all connect with this underlying unity. All life possesses a unique spark of the divine and its potential to create – to bring about harmony, balance and creative beauty into the world, which are essential facets of any healthy spirituality. For within us there is the creative divine impulse, and when we create, we are taking part in and celebrating the creativity that exists within the universe – we become co-creators. Matthew Fox brings this to our attention in his seminal work *Original Blessing*:

> *Here lies the deepest of all meaning behind cosmogenesis, the unfolding birth of the cosmos, and here we, as co-creators with God, have so significant a role to play. It is here that all art, all work, all self-expression, all sexuality, all creativity, all the divine powers of the human who is royal [born with powers to unfold the greatest of all spiritual potential] find its fullest expression. The birthing of our life as a life of beauty and a work of art is necessarily a birth of God in the cosmos.*

This universal call of our spiritual nature involves finding a healthy balance between being and becoming, embracing mindful deeds, moments of quiet reflection, peaceful stillness, compassionate actions, *healthy* non-attachment (which does not imply an unimpassioned state of being, but being unbound by any restrictive feelings or mental states) and helping, whenever we can, to bring about justice, unity and equality into the world. The word non-attachment is replaced in some schools, such as psychosynthsis psychology, with the term *disidentify*, as it draws our attention to how we associate with things we become attached to and lose ourselves in false perceptions of our authentic nature.

Without discovering ways to be still, reflective, peaceful and in tune with life, we can never be fully present when we are with others, or be able to tap into greater realms of creativity, love and just actions – our well of kindness will not be replenished enough for us to act as compassionately as we could. Unless we know how to reflect on living, find our spiritual centre, accept life's various textures and work towards discovering expanded levels of awareness, we will not be able to find a lasting contentment, be truly effective in what we do, or become adequately conscious of wider plateaus of being. "Until humankind extends its circle of compassion to all living things, it will not itself find peace", the eco-philosopher Albert Schweitzer firmly believed.

The way of the artist

Wholesome creativity, which should not be confused with egocentric ideas of creativity, is a natural and integral part of spirituality. To neglect creative and skilful parts of ourselves – meaning not only those that we may think of as being traditional artistic pursuits – means neglecting the infinite variety of gifts that God has blessed us with. The New Testament reminds us of this, when it mentions the different gifts allotted to each of us by God's grace (Romans 12.6). It is what the word *grace* is primarily about: divine abilities that we have been blessed with to use.

The ultimate gifts are those which reshape our being, and

lead us to emotional and mental maturity – to the birthing of the fruits of wisdom and compassion and their continuous growth, to learning how to tread lightly upon Earth, live peacefully, purify our minds, hearts and awareness and perform spontaneous acts of kindness. The artistic impulse within us takes on deeper meaning when creative acts are performed as expressions of spiritual living and a recognition of our unity with others. Such acts are performed with compassionate purpose and always possess a sense of selflessness about them, and flow healthily from us when there is an openness to and a profound and deep understanding of life.

But it should be mentioned that although various forms of art and creativity involve right-brain intuitive thinking, it does not imply that left-brain activity is unimportant. This is something that can be misunderstood when spirituality is interpreted as only being about the creative side of the brain. The engagement of study and continuous learning can all play their part in shaping a wider and more flexible outlook and bringing about more depth in our abilities. Without such things as social and global awareness, Matthew Fox reminds us in *Original Blessing*, an artist can lack the essential tools needed for her or his craft to address relevant topics that speak to people about their current age. The importance of this is not only connected with our general understanding of what it is to be artistic, but is also linked with the *wholeness* of everyone's growth – with the potential to be spiritually active in daily life and know intuitively what paths to take and decisions to make. For intuition without knowledge can often lack healthy direction and focus.

This supreme art emerges as a result of our interactive relationship with the cosmic dance of creation, in its quest for universal harmony. It supplies us with an infinite variety of possibilities and potential that can be awakened to, and leads us to an awareness of every moment being sacred – to an active form of spirituality that is intrinsically bound-up with a realisation of wholeness, and the natural flow of compassion that works through us as a result of understanding our connection with all.

Because of this interrelation, we have an individual and collective responsibility, not only for humanity, but for all life, as we are all one family, created in God, with infinite positive potential to achieve spiritual greatness. We all possess the power to touch other lives and manifest essential gifts, such as kindness, empathy, humility, joy in others' accomplishments, friendship, the sharing of happiness, selflessness, and caring about and helping in the creative process of human and non-human life, even in the smallest of activities. These gifts are found in all moments when we are fully present to life, have set aside self-centred concerns and connect deeply with the holiness of living (the word *holy* is a traditional word for *wholeness*).

Spiritual gifts
Our current age beckons us to find healthy ground, and to respect the equality and rights of every species. One essential thread running through all traditions that has the capacity to unite, heal and overcome barriers, is the practice of selfless acts of compassion and truly caring about other people and life. In

both Matthew's and Mark's Gospel, Jesus is said to have cursed the tree that did not bear fruit. The blossoming of fruitful actions, such as the practice of loving kindness and skilful daily life conduct are central tenets of the Buddhist tradition. In Islam, charity is one of its five pillars. There is often work done for the poor and sick in all spiritual traditions. When there is not, the branch of that tradition is never as rich as the branches that do. An essential ingredient has been misplaced, because of a lack of a kind heart.

"Whoever does not have love does not know God, for God is love", John's Gospel points out (7:8). The Old Testament also reminds us to, "love our neighbour as our self" (Leviticus 19:18), which the Jewish people are called to live and Jesus advocated as the second greatest commandment, after loving God with all one's heart, mind and soul (Matthew 22:37-39). Wayne Teasdale succinctly informed us that,

We have been given the gift of life in this perplexing world to become who we ultimately are: creatures of boundless love, caring compassion, and wisdom.

The word *agape* is used in Christian spirituality, in relation to performing unconditional love, as was seen in the charitable work of Mother Teresa. For many years now there has been a growing healthy interest in *Engaged Buddhism*, which focuses on practical social activism and aims to bring about positive changes in various communities and countries. The different Yoga paths focus on cultivating wisdom, wholesome intentions, fulfilling one's social obligations, selfless work and loving all as expressions of the divine. A popular prayer from Jewish scripture calls upon God to establish peace, goodness, blessings, graciousness, kindness and compassion upon us all and upon the people of Israel. The prophetic message of Micah in the Bible, reminds us that every individual has an obligation to both God and her or his community to act justly, be merciful and walk humbly with God (6:8).

When we spend time talking with people from different cultures and spiritual traditions, we discover that just about everyone seems to know inherently that if the central message of these teachings were fully embraced and were wholesomely expressed as a part of everyone's being, the world would naturally become a more loving, caring and peaceful place. Martin Luther King Jr. prophetically reminded us that ultimately, "The choice is between nonviolence and nonexistence."

BUILDING CREATIVE
COMMUNITIES

*I do not think the measure of a civilization is how tall
its buildings of concrete are, but rather how well its
people have learned to relate to their environment
and fellow human beings.*

– SUN BEAR OF THE CHIPPEWA TRIBE

To understand creative spirituality is to understand our
connection to the divine and to realise how it is ultimately
seeking to express itself in and through all that we do. We
in fact already possess all that we need to be in a productive
interactive relationship with the divinity of the universe;
we only have to find the intuitive insight that is called for
to overcome the appearance of separation from it. When we
can do this, we bring our lives into balance with the creativity
that lies and is inherent within us, and open ourselves to the
evolving and transforming power of spiritual growth, which is
constantly seeking to encourage us to participate in building
nurturing, harmonious and caring communities on Earth. This
includes building a global conscious spirituality and a united
Earth community.

On this subject, the American writer, Buddhist, spiritual

teacher and psychologist, Jack Kornfield, pointed out that, "community is created, not when people come together in the name of religion, but when they come together bringing honesty, respect, and kindness to support an awakening of the sacred."

When we listen to people's feelings about spirituality, it becomes clear that many are disillusioned with organised religions and more traditional religious routes and beliefs, especially when considering the more fundamentalist strands exhibiting extreme acts of violence and holding on to out-dated concepts and morals that have little relevance to contemporary life – such as the age of Earth, a denial of evolution, and ancient prejudices about sexuality and gender – and being unable to accept the diversity of global society. Religions have at various times caused some of the greatest divisions in the world and been more concerned with exerting authority, power and exclusivity, rather than promoting authentic spiritual values, such as an inclusion of all people and encouraging creative thinking and unity. In *Power, Freedom and Grace*, Deepak Chopra mentions,

What the world calls power *is really fear that leads to manipulation and control of others, which in turn leads to violence and suffering. Real power is the power to create, the power to transform, the power to heal, and the power to be free. Real power comes from our connection to our deepest self, to what is real.*

Unity in diversity

Although some contemporary thinkers have tried to separate

religion from spirituality, there is little hope of finding real harmony this way. There is a need to accept people as they are and to realise that religious belief can also be a unifying force that encompasses and cares for all and, therefore, a spiritual force in human life. The majority of people are not going to abandon their faiths and important practices that bring them together, which means we have to look for more accepting and respectful ways in which we can harmoniously live with diversity and find mutually beneficial enrichment. In fact spiritual growth is always more fruitful when it is able to accept different perspectives on life and living.

Learning how to agree to disagree without feeling insecurely challenged by another's point of view, is an essential facet of any form of spiritual maturity. In *The Dignity of Difference*, Rabbi Jonathan Sacks highlights this point, as well as the dangers of unthought through universal ideals that do not allow for individuality, nor accept diversity.

Sometimes we find people seeking to promote the notion of 'everyone singing from the same hymn book'. If this implies a genuine inclusiveness and caring for all, it will move forward with compassion and achieve great things that are needed for our current age. On the other hand, if it means focusing on just a single area of interest, or wanting to see everything that some might wish to classify as *spiritual* as positive, and all things under the heading of *religious* as negative, we will need to question how useful such ideas would be, as it is not always easy to separate one category from another, and say that this is where one thing ends and another begins. It could also leave the door open to an unnatural balance of power, with a belief in there being only one true point of view that cannot be questioned, which would discourage free thinking, a spiritually mature acceptance of difference and the wisdom which is within everyone to be genuinely appreciated and encouraged to grow.

A healthy way forward is multifaceted and interspiritual, and includes acquiring a world-centric vision, awakening to *inclusive* universal realms of divinity, and growing beyond the boundaries that separate us. Within this there is obviously a call for deep ecumenical and interfaith work that helps us to accept those with different perspectives and beliefs to our own, overcome prejudices and discover joy and spiritual growth in the new and fertile ground we can share.

I find it sad that in today's world someone as respected as Jonathan Sacks had to retract a statement from one of his books about no single tradition having a monopoly on spiritual truth. For God does not speak only through one religion. Most of us have friends, relatives, neighbours and working colleagues from different faiths, and our lives are enriched by our diversity, beliefs and cultures. Putting energy into any form of spirituality that separates itself from important life empowering teachings and practices in people's lives, will obviously be limited in what it can achieve.

A greater wisdom

Throughout human history there have been various teachers who have sought to widen the boundaries of their tradition and be more all-embracing – to include not only those from other belief systems and none, but also to seek ways in which to include various levels of spiritual being, including the physical, mystical, shamanistic, psychic and psychological realms that link us with different spheres of knowledge and experience. Healthy changes we see happening today are, to a certain degree, a switch to lost ways of thinking about spirituality. Instead of viewing the divine as predominantly transcendent and possessing only masculine qualities, there has been a shift to acknowledging and opening to divinity as omnipresent and panentheistic (in the workings of Nature, as well as beyond it), with attributes of the creative and compassionate divine feminine – with qualities of the heart. Instead of running from Nature, we need to embrace and include her as part of the spiritual journey. For all things and creatures are unique expressions of the divine. "Gaze into the heart of each creature and kin and behold the Beloved who gazes upon you with love", Sister Georgene Wilson tells us.

Although traditionally there has invariably been these two principal ways of thinking about the divine, it has been the idea of God outside of the universe that has become the most predominant in the Judaeo, Christian and Islamic traditions, which has overshadowed the creative Earth Mother and cosmic forms of divinity. Yet our Earth could never have come into being without the creative workings of the universe and is still evolving and constantly relying on its interaction with the surrounding solar system to sustain her. Our planet is, therefore, interwoven with cosmic realms of creativity and with a profound universal consciousness that contemporary *open minded* western theists would now accept as a divinely superconscious activity, instead of a soulless machine that has been left to run on its own energy.

Celebrating life

Thinking of God as predominantly transcendent and outside of the universe (a duality reinforced by Newtonian science and Descartian philosophy from the 17th century onwards) is now seen as one of the prime influences on humankind's general lack of concern for the natural world. Seeing it as being something to disassociate from has also not helped, which both eastern and western teachings have encouraged at times. On the other hand, recognizing an omnipresent divine spirit, which has the power to awaken us to the wonder and awe of life, and finding ways that we can benefit one another and the abundance of life around us is a more holistically healthy, all-encompassing compassionate path to take. Instead of a split between the physical world and the world of the spirit, we reconnect with the all-ness of existence and its rich diversity, as it truly is.

This cannot be achieved by seeing the world too literally as an illusion – as some branches of Hindu Vedanta philosophy and schools of Mahayana Buddhism have occasionally promoted – and therefore something to be denied, or thought of as negative in some way, which can lead to caring little about Nature and physical life.

We may have misperceptions of physical existence, but this does not imply it is a total illusion, but that we are not seeing things as they really are. A celebration of life on Earth is needed – to see it as an interrelated and unified sacred whole, with profound meaning and purpose, which, if we are open enough to embrace it, can enrich and transform our lives in every instant. The Vietnamese Zen Buddhist monk and teacher, Thich Nhat Hanh, who teaches about *interbeing*, our interdependence with all, also reminds us about the miraculousness of every moment and being aware of the beauty of the world around us:

> *Everyday we are engaged in a miracle which we don't even recognize: a blue sky, white clouds, green leaves, the black curious eyes of a child – our own two eyes. All is a miracle.*

THE POWER OF INTENTION

Whatever a person sows he or she shall reap.

– GALATIANS

I f we unfold actions that are authentic expressions of the spirit, which aim to benefit all people and species, we will discover ways of making the world a more loving and harmonious place. In a holistic and an integral approach to spirituality, nothing is left out – everything becomes a part of the evolving and growing process. This includes looking at our individual selves, our social interactions and working through essential stages of development. It aims for a harmonisation and an integration of both the emotional and intellectual parts of ourselves, seeks justice for the oppressed, and celebrates diversity in different people, cultures and life.

Cultivating wholesome development

It is unfortunate that religious and spiritual traditions can become complacent and lose something of their original radical message. It is why schisms sometimes happen, as there can be an impetus felt to shake things up and reassess a tradition's focus. Instead of believing we have all the answers, spiritual and religious beliefs need to lead us to *asking more questions* about what we truly value, believe, and the accepted norms of life and conduct. There is an apt saying about preferring to be Socrates dissatisfied and searching for answers, than complacent and unaware of wider realms of spirituality. We must ask ourselves, 'What is important *now*?' 'What is going to be useful for us to move forward in our growth and live in harmony with the greater world?'

If we only find peace with those who think the same as we do, we will find ourselves denying much of our spiritual potential. There are important plateaus of development where we connect with wider realms of experience, with those outside of our regular circles of friends and comfort zones, and realise the collective responsibilities we share for humanity and other species.

Actions have consequences
Indian traditions tell us much about karmic actions – how unskilful actions cause us to suffer, and how skilful ones help to heal our wounds, forgive, be whole, balanced and in tune with the wider world around us. Teachings about karma are concerned with how everyday experience can condition us into being a certain way and believing that we are a particular type of person, with likes and dislikes and fixed character traits. If we think of what we valued and focused our lives around ten to fifteen years ago, we will see that many of the things we currently identify with and consider as being a part of who we are, are not as fixed as we thought.

Parts of our nature will be healthy, wholesome and

beneficial to the growth of our overall being, whereas others may be the opposite. We will often possess qualities that inhibit us from discovering and displaying our true nature, which need to be recognized, owned and transformed in order for us to move forward healthily and be open to the richness of life.

Deep-rooted negatives (called *samskaras* in the Yogic traditions) can be a particular problem, as they continually supply us with inhibiting patterns. This is where practices of awareness and mindfulness come in, and becoming conscious of what yogis, yoginis and psychologist call the important silent *observer/witness consciousness*, which supplies us with a window into the depths of our being, and helps us to be watchful in the garden of our awareness in order to cultivate beneficial seeds for spiritual growth. This is not about being aloof and detached, but being fully awake to the many choices we have in life. It is in many ways a gradual expanding and unfolding process, which seeks out spiritual living every step of the way to finding peace and at onement with life in each moment.

In Indian traditions, the word *karma* literally means *action* and is linked with the understanding of actions having consequences. Over the centuries, key beliefs about karma have been linked with various teachings, such as whether a person fulfils her or his assigned duties, takes steps to avoid harming others, is devoted to God or undertakes harsh ascetic practices. In Buddhism, different Upanishads and the Yoga Sutra, skilful and unskilful karmic actions are linked with desires and ethical conduct – the intentions behind actions – as well as meditation practices. In early Buddhist commentaries, there is a list of five categories of natural law that are said to influence us, of which karma is only *one* (number 4). They are:

1. Physical objects and changes in the environment.

2. Heredity.

3. The workings of the mind.

4. Human behaviour.

5. The interrelation and interdependence of all things.

Further to these are the laws of society, which can influence human thought and behaviour and so link with teachings about karma and how we can achieve spiritual progress in our development. We see from these laws that not everything is necessarily bound up with some past karmic action or influence being played out, which western thinkers sometimes mistakenly believe. It is also worth considering Carl Jung's teachings about the collective unconscious, which suggest there are other influences at play within the world. Viewed psychologically, karma is nothing mysterious, but basic common sense about unhealthy states of mind causing us to suffer and behave in less compassionate ways. Thich Nhat Hanh points this out in *The Heart of the Buddha's Teachings*:

*Every time a [negative] seed is watered ... we will suffer and
make the people we love suffer at the same time....*
*If the positive seeds in us grow stronger day and night,
we will be happy and we will make the people we love happy.*

Linking with karmic influences, is the mention of three types
of action in both the Hindu and Jain tradition (called the *three
gunas/qualities*). They are mentioned in many of Hinduism's
most sacred books, including the Bhagavad Gita, which
advocates an active and a devotional path of spirituality. Satish
Kumar highlighted their environmental implications in his
book *Spiritual Compass*.

Although the *gunas* can be interpreted in different ways
and are seen to interact continually with each other, at their
most basic of psychological levels, they can be looked upon as
the following descriptions:

1. Actions that create harmony, are responsible, balanced,
mindful and pure, flow spontaneously and freely from
our nature, and connect with and consider others and the
environment (*sattvic* actions).

2. Actions that are influenced by self-centred desires, which
cause a strain on our relationships with others and the
environment, and arise from a belief in self-importance
(*rajasic* actions).

3. Actions that are performed from a confused, unclear and
unthought through state of mind, which are irresponsible,

have little consideration for the outcome, cause offence, and harm other people and life (*tamasic* actions).

From a spiritual standpoint we can see how the more negative actions summarised above, would need transforming and how the cultivation of *sattvic* actions are spiritually beneficial. It is when we recognize we can all display degrees of these qualities at different times in our lives that we take the important step of owning both our positives and negatives and finding ways of healthily interacting with life. Becoming aware of negatives becomes a positive action, because through this we start to awaken to healthier growth and uncover transforming realms of spirituality that are beneficial to life.

The essential call of spiritual work is interwoven with practical living and actions that bring benefit to others. In Ranchor Prime's *Vedic Ecology* he describes how,

> ... *planting trees and digging wells have traditionally been the two great acts of charity by which everyone could earn merit and universal appreciation. Trees such as mango, neem or banyan were planted along roads to give shelter and shade, their leaves acting as natural air conditioners. Beneath their broad canopies generations of wayfarers, stopping for a rest or meal, have found relief.*

Ranchor Prime also mentions how trees are not only seen as sacred and having spirits dwelling within them by the Indian people and how they, along with plants, have healing properties, but are also a direct link to India's great teachers of the past, as the teachers originally inhabited India's great forests and imparted their wisdom in them.

Spiritual precepts

People such as the German psychoanalyst and psychiatrist Karen Horney believed in having *no shoulds*, which has become a popular idea with some students and teachers, where either a single metaphysical or an existential ideal is advocated instead. Although spiritual actions are related to a receptive response to our finer qualities, *shoulds* and *should nots* are still found as basic codes of conduct in many religions.

Though some of these may be questionable as to whether they are relevant or not to contemporary life, there are some that are essential in regards to matters of taking responsibility for our actions and not harming others. On the one hand we may feel that we do not need to be reminded about such principles, but on the other it would be foolish to abandon their advocation. All areas of human life actually have codes of conduct, which when ignored often lead to a breakdown in any worthy sense of trust or harmony. We only have to listen to the news to see that there is a violent mentality and short-sighted selfishness growing in many cultures. Although there are reasons why this is happening, *which need to be addressed*, it also means that we require basic laws, principles, sanctions and codes of behaviour to protect the innocent, whether human or non-human victims of what is happening in our societies. To actually say, 'We should not have any shoulds', is a contradiction that overlooks basic realities of what is needed to make the world a safer place.

There are always difficulties when we try to take a reductionist, flatland route to spiritual matters instead of a multi-dimensional one and leave out important areas, such as taking care of people's basic needs, which helps to ease tensions in society, and promoting non-violent actions, whether towards other people or other life forms.

In E. F. Schumacher's best selling *Small is Beautiful*, he mentions that we need different levels of understanding – what he calls *grades of significance* – otherwise we will not be able to make sense of the world or our place in the universe. Importantly Seyyed Hossein Nasr points out that teachings which accept different grades of being (different levels of awareness and stages of development) do not undermine beliefs in an essential oneness or non-duality:

> *The multiple states of being do not negate the oneness of Being at all. For all levels there is but the radiance of the one Face of the Beloved: there is ultimately but a single Divine Reality.*

Within all spiritual paths, there are essential practices for everyday living, such as the *yamas* (external ethical virtues) and *niyamas* (the cultivation of inner virtues) in the Yogic traditions, which include non-harmfulness, truthfulness and mindful introspection. As a whole, the *yamas* and *niyamas* are looked upon as indispensable within the various Yogic paths. In the sacred writings of Sikhism, it is reported that its first guru, Guru Nanak, was asked about *ahimsa* (non-violence), to which he replied:

Do not wish evil for anyone. This is ahimsa *of thought.*
Do not speak harshly of anyone. This is ahimsa *of speech.*
Do not obstruct anyone's work. This is ahimsa *of action.*
If a man speaks ill of you, forgive him.
Practise physical, mental and spiritual endurance.
Help the suffering even at the cost of your life.

Yet contemporary life presents us with dilemmas that teachers such as the historical Buddha, Jesus and Guru Nanak did not have to face in their Earthly lifetimes, such as when someone's work involves destroying the world's ancient rain forests, or growing single crops over vast areas that weaken Nature's biodiversity. Just as life is always changing, so too must our spiritual understanding in order to act justly, responsibly and appropriately for our time.

ORIGINAL GOODNESS

*There is not one person who does not have
the capacity to be a Buddha.*

– THICH NHAT HANH

The advocation of introspection and mindfulness, which is encouraged in all healthy spiritual traditions, helps us to become aware of any unhelpful, deep rooted patterns that have formed, such as restrictive negative thoughts, feelings, impulses or actions that can affect various states of spiritual awareness. This is part of the classic *know thy self* wisdom that is so important, which if overlooked can cause problems later on in development. It has been well recognized within the last 30 years how psychological work is needed to accompany healthy spiritual growth. The saying, "You have to become someone before you become no one", comes to mind here, and refers to doing necessary ground work, instead of avoiding it by escaping into practices and beliefs, in an attempt to bliss out and deny any problems that might need acknowledging, letting in and working through to achieve a balanced wholeness of being. The American psychologist, John Welwood, has popularly termed this form of avoidance, *spiritual bypassing.*

With the dedication to bring about a transformation of our overall selves, we can change inhibiting traits. For only the present moment exists and how we respond to each passing moment, thought and experience is primarily a matter of free will, choice and individual responsibility. An essential part of this is about having a flexible will that can adapt creatively to situations, as well as the cultivation of present moment awareness, along with a pure mind and heart with wholesome intentions.

Interestingly, quantum physicists have noticed how electrons, which are one of the most basic components of matter, start acting differently when we observe them. They start behaving like particles (tiny balls of energy) instead of like waves, which they normally do when we are not observing them. This implies that matter changes when we focus our attention on and interact with it and that we are influencing our physical surroundings with our directed thoughts. It reminds us about the power of the mind and demonstrates that it is not only our physical actions that can bring about positive changes in the world, which is nothing new of course, as millions of people have believed in and have been using the power of prayer for thousands of years.

Seeds of transformation
Any exercises, such as the cultivation of a kind heart, skilful social engagement, meditation, artistic work, therapeutic reflections, affirmations, Earth centred rituals, mantra, or

contemplative prayer, that help us to achieve healthy states of being, are obviously important and need to be essential ingredients in numerous forms of spiritual practice. Any of these can be powerful tools for transforming negatives – including low self-esteem and nonchalant attitudes towards life – as they can help us to focus more on inherent positive qualities.

Progress to mature growth requires working with the good, moderate and shadow parts of ourselves – realising realms of pure being and transforming anything that restricts us from reflecting the more authentic spiritual self and connecting with life in more wholesome ways. If we are open and honest with ourselves, we will recognize how facets of our psychological nature influence us at different times, and that we are continually changing in the ways that we think, feel and act.

The road forward is not to deny the different shades and textures of our nature, but to recognize the journeys and our individual stories that have brought us to this moment – to understand why we are the way we are and why we sometimes act in ways that we feel are in conflict with our spiritual nature. There are often good reasons why we sometimes have to pick ourselves up when we stumble. Often it is because we are suffering mentally, physically or emotionally to some degree. Often it is because we feel our spiritual nature is not being allowed to surface and express itself in supportive environments. It is here that we can start to ask ourselves questions about why we feel and act in certain ways and what can be done to help us move forward and bring about positive changes.

It is sensible not to impose unrealistic demands on our lives and hold spiritual ideals that no one could possibly live up to, but to be realistic and accept our complete selves – to embrace the whole of our being, be gentle about our misgivings and bring about a natural unfoldment and a recognition of the awe inspiring transforming power of our spiritual nature. Negatives are never true reflections of who we are. Beneath them there is infinite creative potential seeking to express itself. Allowing our deeper spiritual being to commune profoundly with us leads to a harmonisation of all parts into a balanced whole.

This process involves letting our barriers down, and allowing ourselves to be more open, loving and caring – to both ourselves and others. But for this to happen, we will often have to have contact with a healthy community of friends and people around us, as becoming more aware means opening to more sensitive and vulnerable areas, which we may need guidance in knowing how to handle. We will, therefore, need a supportive network of people who are understanding about the changes we are bringing about. If we are not members of such a community, it is wise to consider finding like-minded people who we can travel with on our spiritual journey.

There can also be a swing to Dark Night of the Soul experiences after intensive creative work, or when wider realms of spiritual experience are realised. Both of which I have noticed within my own growth and creativity at times. Such episodes are quite common on the mystical path and have been widely written about by both contemporary and early teachers of spirituality. They can often seem like spiritually dry periods that are seldom lit by any up-lifting experience, often interspersed with episodes of everyday life taking on negative interpretations, but are also times of letting go, letting be and surrendering self-centred desires and goals.

It is also not uncommon for students to go through stages where they become less patient and more emotionally raw, because they have become more aware of what is going on within and around them and because people are not supporting them in the fresh perspectives of spirituality they are waking up to – their recognition of new areas for wholesome growth. This is where experienced guidance is often called for, as well as an unfoldment of one's own wisdom and insight, in order to discern what is the best way forward, steer around the inevitable trouble spots and find courage to stand by one's convictions. It is because we have entered a new landscape that we are unfamiliar with that these difficult openings and times of spiritual crisis happen. Stanislav and Christina Grof coined the phrase *spiritual emergency* to describe such phenomena and some counsellors are experienced in this area.

Students who can stand back serenely from entangled or restrictive situations and see them for what they are with an equanimous state of mind, will often find the best solutions to problems. However, this does not imply feeling bad about ourselves if we cannot achieve this. We have our human side, just as much as anyone else, and need to reassure ourselves that we are trying in our own way to make headway into spiritual heartlands and awaken to a greater awareness.

Embracing the good in all

When we are truly at one with ourselves and the spiritual core of our being, life starts to speak to us in fresh and dynamic ways that are not tied to old restrictive patterns of thinking and behaviour. As we open to our authentic selves – our spirit, our atman, our Buddha Nature, our original goodness – we participate more freely and skilfully in all activities of life. We start to include all areas of living and realise we are not separate from vast oceans of life around us. Through this holistic embrace comes a true awakening to the various realms of our psychic and physical being and a deep sense of connection to life, as we realise that all things touch our lives and are intrinsic parts of who we are.

The ways to discovering and expressing this deep level of spirituality are many. Traditional artistic routes involve dancing, singing, painting, sculpting, writing, drumming and story telling, as found and practised in many cultures. Whether we are artist, shamans, carpenters, students, nurses, teachers, labourers, activists, priests or healers, there are numerous subtle and profound ways of making our daily actions a dedication to skilful, wholesome, compassionate, fair and just living. "Each tree is recognized by its own fruit", Jesus is reported to have said in Luke's Gospel (6:44). "A person's true wealth is the good he does in this world", the prophet Muhammad reminded us.

The diagram on the opposite page was inspired by one I came across in A. Parthasarathy's *The Eternities*, and shows areas of life that overlap and interact with each other (including a *healthy understanding* of our individual self), which need to be integrated within our awareness of all things within and around us.

Of additional interest is the term *ecological self* that was coined by the influential Norwegian philosopher and one of the founders of the Deep Ecology Platform, Arne Naess. It connects with areas of the diagram and involves transcending restrictive levels of self-interest in order to embrace a wider circle of eco-friendly spirituality.

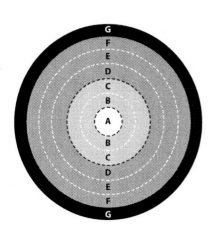

A. Individual self: mind, body and feelings (including the individual psychological self).

B. Family, friends and acquaintances (people we know and have contact with).

C. Local community.

D. Global community.

E. All beings and species.

F. Earth (including its air, rivers, seas, mountains, etc.).

G. The Universe (including Earth and our solar system).

☐ (A) The Individual Earth Self.
☐ (B-C) The Social Earth Self.
▨ (D-E-F) The Wider Earth Self.
■ (G) The Cosmic/Universal Self.

REALMS OF
POTENTIAL

CHAPTER
SIX

*Progress is impossible without change; and those who
cannot change their minds cannot change anything.*

        – GEORGE BERNARD SHAW

E very age witnesses change as new discoveries are made
and communities intermingle with those from other
cultures. Fundamentalists become defensive, instead of
embracing changes and others from outside of their closed
circles. We in fact can all become defensive to what is new,
fresh and often needed, when we feel it threatens the things we
believe. But without change, there is little chance for healthy
growth. With our current exchange of cultures, what are
possibly called for are new Renaissance and Enlightenment
periods, though the last Renaissance Europe had is now
thought to have been over romanticised. The writer on and
teacher of Integral Spirituality, Steve McIntosh, believes we
are already entering a second Enlightenment period. Ideally,
such periods in history only flourish when all the arts and
sciences are explored in an open minded spirit of mutual
worth and appreciation.

    Currently, for good or ill, our contemporary societies

are witnessing great transformations. Ideas of spirituality, morality, psychology and science have all affected the way we live and view the world. Most of us do not even view life in the same way that our parents did when they were our age. Some cultures have started to fight against this and are returning to what they see as traditional values. At the moment we do not have the right balance. There is a call for a re-evaluation of what is truly needed in order to go forward and a need for us to be open to the richness of wisdom, goodness and creativity that can be found in all cultures.

There are immense treasures in all the great wisdom traditions. We live in multi-cultural societies and are surrounded by people from different faiths. If we do not seek to understand our global neighbours, look for common ground and accept diversity, then we will never find lasting peace in the world or our development. Active forms of spirituality find harmony by being inclusive. Equally, we need to be receptive to contemporary knowledge that widens our perceptions of life.

Authentic growth is obviously not self-centred or only focused on a narrow circle of interest, but an ongoing organic process that continually expands to encompass all as a profound spiritual synthesis. When our development includes others, we open to the richness of their wisdom, goodness and creativity.

Oneness with all
Instead of being separate and *apart*, everything is inter-connected and *a part* of us, and we are a part of everyone

and everything. The creatures of the world's jungles and the African plains, the sacred Earth beneath our feet and the sky above our heads, all share an interdependent relationship with our being, just as much as we share an interdependent relationship with them.

Although life and the universe are popularly seen as mechanistic and as being pushed towards a pointless future (a concept that is in fact at least a hundred years out of date with contemporary scientific thinking), our experience of Nature tells us something quite different. Most of us hold a deep seated recognition that it is both creative and evolving, and that our lives are deeply interwoven with the fabric of this activity.

When we consider the existence of all things, we can see how there are many causes linked with bringing them fully into being. Human birth, until recently, has required two parents to join together in a sexual embrace, and regular food and clothing produced by Nature and numerous people throughout the globe, help to sustain us and keep us warm. Simply being alive has required nearly fourteen billion years of the universe's history for us to be here at this moment in time. The implications of this are vast and this alone ought to lead us to appreciate all life and people – including our own unique individuality.

Keeping within the great wisdom traditions' understanding of spirituality, Shakti Gawain pointed out how connecting with life and others is grounded in a profound connection to our own being:

Ultimately, what we are looking to is the deepest connection within ourselves. As we get more connected to that, we begin to feel in harmony with other people and with the rest of the world.

Qualities of authentic nature

When we openly contemplate the workings and beauty of Nature, the tiniest of creatures or the smallest of plants can open us to deeper mysteries. Such openings are interconnected cores of spiritual and mystical insight, in which there is a need for an integration of what is realised. The world's spiritual traditions remind us of this and often highlight that it is not enough to just experience wider states of awareness, but that we should also embody and live their implications. For if *all* is part of us and we are part of *the all*, it then follows that every creature and species is a member of our universal family, and just as we feel a sense of connection to and naturally care about the welfare of our closest blood family members, there is a need to be in touch with realms of our being that include and care for our global brothers and sisters. It is the realisation of this reality that beckons and requires us to work towards discovering and putting into action, such as becoming actively involved in the welfare of all species (including the human species) and protecting Nature's biodiversity.

Within all the great wisdom traditions there are central teachings about this, and for finding peace, equanimity and cultivating finer qualities of love, empathy and goodness, which are essential attributes of our original nature. Ramana Marharshi pointed out that, "The Ultimate Truth is so simple; it is nothing more than being in one's natural, original state." The Gospel of Thomas encourages a realisation of the kingdom of God within and all around us. Daoists masters wisely remind us about *living with the Dao*. This highlights finding a natural flow and balance in everyday activities and being at one with the creative *chi* energies found in all life. For every being is, "an expression of the Dao", Lui I-Ming tells us. Following such wisdom becomes a matter of opening to the sacredness of, and the potential to create in, each moment – to awaken to that which is paradoxically the same in, as well as the uniqueness of, all and the spiritual work, such as natural and spontaneous acts of kindness and compassion, that flow from being in harmony with the continual creative energy of a profoundly spiritual life.

Communing with the spirit
When spiritual experience encompasses harmonising opposing parts of our being, we become more congruent and find ways and healthy solutions for healing conflicts, both within us and around us. But it needs to be mentioned that although anyone can have a spiritual opening or experience at any point in her or his journey, these can sometimes be just fleeting moments of awareness. There is, therefore, a requirement for deeper work to be done in order to establish different stages of growth that lead to a greater awareness of life. As Ken Wilber likes to remind us, "States are free, but stages are earned."

The search is always ongoing, which does not imply discarding the wisdom of the past, but being discerning enough to take forward only that which is of value and useful for the growth that lies ahead. "The call" the Christian meditation teacher John Main tells us,

> ... *is to open yourself to your own eternal spirit, to be open to your own rootedness in the Eternal, to start to tread the way, the pilgrimage to fullness of light and fullness of meaning.*

If we are loaded down with too much baggage, we will obviously not be able to travel far. To discover this fullness of light and meaning that John Main describes, where the creative energy of the spirit can work uninhibitedly in and through us, requires letting go of and surrendering our more self-focused interests. The revelation of the spirit communes naturally through us when we do this. Our creativity, which unfolds as a result of this awakening, then becomes an outward expression of revelation, as it connects us with the divine that continually seeks to reveal itself in new acts of inspiration. It touches our emotions, mind and imagination, which helps to enlarge who we are, and leads us to previously unrecognized potential, to discover new realms of possibility. It entices us to move beyond restrictive patterns of belief and behaviour, and to realise that change and growth are always possible.

LOVE OF NATURE

CHAPTER
SEVEN

Love all of God's creation, the whole earth and every
grain of sand in it. Love every leaf, every ray of God's light.
Love the animals, love the plants, love everything.
If you love everything, you will perceive
the divine mystery in things.

– FYODOR DOSTOYEVSKY

The 13th century Christian mystic, Meister Eckhart, wrote that, "We are to love all things that are to lead us to God." If we realise that all things share a collective divinity, it then follows that our love must reach out to include the whole of life, all parts of our psychic being, the world and the evolving universe. Every one of us already seems to possess an innate love for Nature. The contemporary American scientist, Edward O. Wilson, calls this love, *biophilia*. Unfortunately, in more recent centuries, this love for Nature has been overshadowed by humankind's more destructive tendencies, which are destroying much of the world's beauty and delicately balanced ecosystems. All species are unique works of creation and need us to consider ways of protecting them. In *The Creation*, by Edward O. Wilson, he points out how,

... each species, however inconspicuous and humble it may seem to us at this moment, is a masterpiece of biology, and well worth saving.... Prudence alone dictates that we act quickly to prevent the extinction of species and with it, the pauperization of Earth's ecosystems ...

Cherishing all species and our Earth

Every time a species disappears because of our negligence, our Earth becomes less fruitful and diverse in its abundance and consequently, everyone's life becomes less rich. In the search for just *human* after-life and the propagation of purely *human*-centred ethics and morals, many traditions have not focused enough on the protection of all species as an essential ingredient of spirituality. Yet the sea is gradually changing, as some ecologists and representatives of the great spiritual traditions are now beginning to meet and support each other, and are no longer thinking in terms of just human development and unity, and are widening their circles of compassion to embrace the uniqueness of Nature, its incredible diversity and are earnestly considering its needs. For we have to celebrate and treasure all physical life.

In *Befriending the Earth*, Thomas Berry is quoted to have said that, "To wantonly destroy another species is to silence a divine voice forever." When human unfoldment is healthily reflected upon, we realise it cannot be separated from our Earth's or the universe's evolvement. To explore our innate spiritual nature, is to search for deeper dimensions of being and discover a unity and wholeness that is the ground of all activity and existence.

At the most basic levels of life, scientists have discovered there are pure patterns of energy that intertwine and are continuously interacting with each other. Thus we are all intrinsically interrelated, because we all share the same ancestry and energies of life. Every breath we exhale feeds the plants and in return their oxygen feeds us. Our physical bodies are made from the same material that makes stars, plants and other life in the universe. In Tom Atlee's *Reflections on Evolutionary Activism*, he tells us that indigenous people, such as the Australian aborigines, have believed the stars are their ancestors for over a thousand years. Everything is amazingly made up of the same ninety-two naturally occurring elements found in the universe. This means, as Ellen Bernstein reminds us,

> ... *that the earth that we walk upon, the air that we breathe, the food that we eat, are all signs that the world is filled with mystery. Those who cherish this idea sense that everything they encounter is sacred. Nurture this idea, and it will guide the choices you make and the way you live your life.*

Yet, as mentioned, in spite of knowing these incredible facts about our cosmic and interconnected ancestry, many mainstream religions and spiritual movements did not at first move quickly enough to become deeply involved in issues about our planet's ecological problems (even now, there are some who haven't realised the importance of this work), or help to forge a healthy bond between beliefs, evolvement, spiritual practices and caring for the Earth – even though many of the great mystics, such as Teresa of Avila, were only too aware of their relationship with Nature and how it can replenish us:

If we learn to love the earth, we will find labyrinths, gardens, fountains, and precious jewels! A whole new world will open itself to us. We will discover what it means to be truly alive.

While the idea of stewardship is found in both Judaism and Christianity, it only takes us so far, as it implies being left in charge for a period of time while God has somehow disappeared – only to return occasionally or on some future day of judgment. It also implies having dominion over Nature and the Earth, instead of learning how to live peacefully with and caring for and about the natural world. It is when we realise Earth's continuous sacredness and its creation was not something that merely happened billions of years ago and then suddenly stopped, but is still happening and evolving today, that we start to appreciate the wondrous workings of Nature, and consider ways in which we can live in harmony with and fully cherish our home planet.

What is needed is a more *widespread* Earth conscious spirituality that encourages a recognition of our cosmic heritage – one that brings people together from different faiths and none, in a united cause for positive transformations and change. This is not an exclusive spirituality for a selected few, but one in which we are all called to participate equally.

To think of God as having solely masculine attributes, and a spirit world as something purely separate from Nature, is now seen as a contributory influence in humankind's evolvement that has led us to plunder our planet savagely without thinking about the consequences. Destroying Nature damages our kinship with the divine, because the divine permeates and expresses itself through *all* and, so means (as the previous quotation by Thomas Berry pithily implies), when we destroy a species, it diminishes the divine's diverse involvement and expression on Earth.

Living with spiritual purpose

Instead of responsibly interacting with life, humanity as a whole often cuts itself off from healthy engagement with it. In *Waking the Global Heart*, Anodea Judith writes about Duane Elgin, who questioned people from different cultures, such as Japan, India, England and Brazil, and discovered that two thirds of them agreed that humanity is still in its adolescence. Judith goes on to point out how it is easy to see why:

> *We need only turn on the television and to see adolescent behaviour raging through all ages, races, creeds, and genders ... obsessed with our looks, and bursting with teenage libido, we are sorely lacking in social and environmental conscience. We are driven by flashy gadgets and fast changes. We are driven by the whimsy of our desires. Like teenagers cleaning out the refrigerator while entertaining their friends, human populations are insatiably consuming the once vast cupboards of oceans and forests in the attempt to satisfy their voracious appetites.*

Actions such as the above contrast strongly with a spirituality that on one level, acknowledges responsibility, and on another, has purpose and reasons for existing and goes beyond mere self-centred interests. An Earth centred spirituality highlights the latter to achieve a more healthy balance in the ways that we think about life, our development and interactive relationship with Nature and divine levels of being.

Within mainstream scientific thinking and postmodernist philosophy, there still persists negative views about the universe and the natural world, by seeing them as both random and accidental and, therefore, meaningless. There are *no truths*, postmodernist thinkers try to convince us, but then seek to make this idea an absolute itself. Why care about anything and consider spiritual values and practices, such as compassion, nonviolence and selflessly caring about others, when life and Nature are looked upon so negatively? In response to similar ideas in his own lifetime, the writer and satirist, Jonathan Swift, wrote,

> *That the universe was formed by a fortuitous concourse of atoms, I will no more believe than that the accidental jumbling of the alphabet would fall into a most ingenious treatise of philosophy.*

Thankfully not all scientists have a pessimistic outlook on life and have come to recognize the universe's spiritual implications. Some, such as James Lovelock with his insightful observations about Gaia, have observed how our planet is a self-regulating, unifying living organism, which shapes life and *does* in fact appear to have purpose and, therefore, needs to be treated with respect. "Gaia Theory ... challenges the view that the natural world is there to be managed as a resource for human use", Satish Kumar mentions in his book *Spiritual Compass*.

The emergence of organic and human life appear to be no coincidence, as the odds for having the right conditions to create them are billions to one. The physicist Freeman Dyson said that the more he looked at the workings of the universe, the more it seemed clear to him that it knew from the start that humans were coming!

Conscious evolution

When we consider how the living universe came into being, and how it is holistic, integral, interacting and forever in the process of evolving, we realise that it is an important part of who we are, as we are all incredible products of the universe and its awe inspiring creativity. This understanding can unite and lead us to appreciate how divine realms are in the eternal act of creating. And when we create with wholesome intention, we take part in this mystery and creativity, and manifest qualities of our spiritual nature and commune with the divine spirit that permeates all. Our creativity, after all, has its origins in the creative divine mind of the universe that links us intimately with the cosmos and Earth. For Earth, which is full of glorious diversity, activity and colour, has continually stimulated our imaginations, and motivated and inspired us to create in a myriad of different ways for thousands of years.

Deep within most people there is an intuitive knowing that not only life on our planet, but also the universe has a profound interconnected intelligence and purpose, and is being creatively *animated*, instead of meaninglessly *pushed* by the energy left-over from a purely accidental beginning. Of interest is Teilhard de Chardin's mystical omega point, in which he saw the divine drawing all things towards itself to a supreme point of spiritual unity. Whether he was completely right or not perhaps remains to be seen and is a matter of personal belief, though when we think of creation as primarily about continuous evolvement, we see how it is invariably seeking to move forward and find a healthy balance.

Nature mysticism
In spite of what may be on the surface of orthodox western beliefs about God as separate from Nature, if we penetrate the wisdom of various traditions, we will discover that they generally all possess elements of Nature mysticism submerged within them – we find holy wells and mountains, sacred trees and rivers, associated with just about all of them. In Matthew Fox's and Rupert Sheldrake's *Natural Grace*, they mention how this understanding of the sacred appears to be embedded within the human psyche and how there seems to be an essential need for us to relate to the natural world in unique ways, such as pilgrimages to holy places – which interestingly have their own special energies that go beyond set beliefs and attract people from all faiths and none – or rituals that expand our awareness of the sacredness of life.

In fact, any experience of deep contact with Nature often helps in the healing process in times of stress and pain, and leads us to discover wider and more holistic perspectives of life that inevitably enrich us in profound and life enhancing ways.

Doctors have now recognized that simply walking in Nature is one of the best exercises for physical health and mental well-being. As a Londoner I often feel the need to be quiet and spend time in places of beauty, such as Kew Gardens and Epping Forest – which are on the outskirts of London – when the pressures of life make my heart feel heavy.

With the freshness, clarity and insight of a maturing girl's mind, Anne Frank described times amongst Nature and being alone with God, simply and touchingly in her diaries:

The best remedy for those who are afraid, lonely or unhappy is to go outside, somewhere where they can be quiet, alone with the heavens, nature and God. Because only then does one feel that all is as it should be and that God wishes to see people happy, amidst the simple beauty of nature.… I firmly believe that nature brings solace in all troubles.

THE NEXT STAGE
OF THE JOURNEY

CHAPTER
EIGHT

If you are really determined to be on the good side of life,
the forces of the universe are there to help you.
— ROBERT MULLER

Today the rights of non-human species and the preservation of Nature has become one of the highest concerns for a growing number of spiritual seekers. When people first saw colour pictures of Earth taken from outer space, it sparked off numerous environmental movements around the world, because people were so inspired by Earth's beauty, which then influenced them to think more about the importance of global issues and protecting endangered species.

Unfortunately human nature has an annoying habit of becoming complacent with what has become familiar, and constantly searches for something new to experience and become interested in. Yet it is when we know how to be truly present to Earth and Nature that we actually discover they are always changing and renewing themselves in a myriad of different ways and displaying different shades and textures – not only with the seasons, but both are forever in the act of creating new and copious life. Contemporary science and the

Buddhist precept of impermanence also tell us that everything in the universe is forever transforming and in a continual state of change. The saying of the Greek philosopher Heraclitus, about never being able to step into the same stream twice, is profoundly true it seems.

Learning how to live a more simplified and natural life and be in the present moment, helps us to reconnect with Nature. It brings us into contact with deeper realms of being and leads us to recognize the beauty and wonder that is around us. Instead of living in our heads and being bound up in thoughts and self-centred desires that take us some place else, we open to the uniqueness of each moment and the mysteries it reveals. Philip Sherrard also reminds us how being in touch with our own holiness brings us into touch with the world:

> *Once we repossess a sense of our own holiness, we will recover the sense of the holiness of the world.... Only in this way will we once again become aware that our destiny and the destiny of nature are one and the same.*

Replenishing insight

There is often a need for things that replenish us on our journey. This is where a community of like-minded friends, moments and rituals that help us reconnect with life, and activities such as reading and studying can be of great benefit. To dismiss any wisdom is to overlook the creativity of the divine revealing itself in different ways. Just as we find a sense of the sacred in the awe we experience when seeing beauty in a setting sun, there is as much sacred and deep beauty in spiritual insights, teachings and practices that profoundly remind us of our true nature. All activities have merit if followed with compassion and wisdom, and if they help to widen our awareness of what a spiritual life entails.

The ultimate work is about the discovery of our authentic nature and the good that can be done in the world through its influence. Anything that helps us awaken to this is of great value and is why much of the world's great teachings are treated with such respect, because they invariably possess key points about achieving this. In the writings of the Indian sage, Swami Ramdas, he reminds us that,

The key note of a religious life is selfless service – a service born of pure love and compassion for all beings and creatures on this earth.

Spiritual engagement

The one question that many of us must ask ourselves is, 'What is it that makes humans so destructive?' Somewhere along the path of human development, an essential facet of its spiritual roots appears to have been largely forgotten. Wars are obviously one of the worst threats to the world's ecosystems and people's lives and never achieve anything of value.

When we are deeply awake to the sacredness of life, we do not wantonly destroy any living species, just as any responsible parent would not intentionally want to harm their children, but would instead cherish and help them with their growth, and appreciate their individual beauty and abilities. Similarly, just as we would encourage the growth of our own children, we need to cultivate our own creativity and the creativity of others – including other life forms.

This is the opposite of inactivity, as it is within our nature to create, invent, be imaginative and skilful. I find it fascinating that the creation of music was around for millions of years before humans first walked upon Earth, as birds have been composing and singing to each other for much longer than humans and many others creatures. The 20th century French composer Olivier Messiaen, who studied their compositions, noticed how they use precise scales and different tempos and sometimes improvise with each other.

Yet creativity requires us to be responsible for the things we create, as it can be used to wipe out other species, invent torture chambers and weapons of unimaginable devastation, as well as unite and empower people to be more compassionate and seek for justice and equality for all. "Now I am become Death, the destroyer of all worlds", the scientist J. Robert Oppenheimer is reported to have quoted from the Bhagavad Gita, after testing the first atomic bomb.

Encouraging creativity

The power of creativity can be seen in our natural curiosity, which seeks to understand things in order to grow mentally and spiritually, be emotionally mature, more healthily expressive and interact with others in more fruitful ways. An artist can be a person who is sometimes feared, as she or he can shake things up, step outside of the accepted norms and dare to question things from fresher perspectives that others may find difficult to embrace. Creativity is also part of our ability to adapt and survive in times of change and transformation. Creative beauty often comes out of periods of darkness and suffering and helps in the healing process.

Because it is so essential to who we are, we need to be on our guard against any powers or people that seek to dampen our enthusiasm, imagination, vision and energy. For here lies a death of our abilities – of being able to express ourselves in abundantly creative ways. It requires an environment that is open enough to encourage new perspectives, and have the foresight to reach beyond restrictive boundaries and discover that which leads to fertile ground. Any remotely aware person working in education will tell you that building the right environment is an essential ingredient for encouraging individual development. Unfortunately our societies are becoming less supportive and more insular. In the last few decades people as a whole have invested less and less in building supportive communities.

A popularly held answer to our current spiritual crisis, is for our already overstretched schools (which are more about academic achievement and left brain thinking, than encouraging holistic and creative growth) to find ways of fixing much of society's problems. A more realistic route lies in collective responsibility and education, and jointly looking for ways to change wholesomely and become more caring about the creative potential of all people and life and rebuild some of our dysfunctional communities.

One of the biggest influences on society is the popular media, which selectively filters out sensational news about what is happening around the world and rarely supplies positive role models. News channels, web pages and papers, which feed us daily with the ills of contemporary living, negatives about human behaviour, the dysfunctional activities of contemporary celebrities who have become famous for being famous, the shallowness of materialism, competitive sports that split people into separate groups, hardly ever finds room to promote healthy categories of creativity – whether in the form of the traditional arts, or what those in scientific and spiritual fields are doing to promote a more caring Earth community.

The Apollo astronaut, Edgar Mitchell, pointed out that, "We need to make the world safe for creativity and intuition, for it is creativity and intuition that will make the world safe for us." For ultimately our lives are enhanced by creativity, even at the most basic of levels. It gives us all a sense of authentic belonging, which we experience in such things as music, art and places of great beauty that we are drawn to, and has the power to heal divisions and wounds when expressed and opened to in compassionate ways. Matthew Fox points out that,

> We are creators at our very core. Only creating can make us happy, for in creating we tap into the deepest power of self and universe and the Divine Self. We become co-creators, that is, we create with the other forces of society, universe, and the God-self when we commit to creativity.

A new phase of spirituality
From the earliest of archaeological findings, one of the key

activities that defines humans, is the ability to create. Art in recent decades has taken on negative connotation and been associated with consumerism, status, and sometimes seen as a form of psychological sickness. But in its purest form it is an expression of the divine qualities within us and about selflessly serving the communities in which we live. For, "All the talents of God are within you", the great Sufi mystic Hafiz reminded us. The artists involved in the building of many of the world's great temples, churches, mosques and cathedrals, created them more out of love of their craft and what they believed in, and were inspired by this as a way of contributing to their communities.

Having a creative and creation centred spirituality is obviously not the same as having an egocentric materialistic outlook. It is a spirituality that thinks of new ways of healthily relating to the world that is all around and has brought us to this critical moment in history. It is a path that awakens us to our unique position on Earth and the changes we can put into place for positive steps forward – changes which will enable the advances needed for actualising profound levels of interaction with different realms of life, based on the realisation that we live, move and have our being in an evolving spiritual universe. This is more than just a mere knowing, but a state of being that is authentically lived.

Yet there will be no actual time in this when we can say that we have arrived at the ultimate truth or journey's end. It is something that is forever created in each moment and action – an awareness of the present where *the all* becomes central to our development. Because of this, a healthy spontaneity and flexibility to the inevitable twists and turns of life, and our interdependent relationship with others and the world around us are important, as well as being able to cultivate any potential abilities that may be required to live compassionately with purpose.

In the writings of Thomas Berry, he refers to essential levels of development such as this, as being important for what he called the *Ecozoic Era* – a crucial period where outmoded, unharmonious and no longer helpful states of being that create harmful divisions between people and the wider natural world are shed:

> *This new, emergent phase of Earth history can be defined as that period when humans would be present to the Earth in a mutually enhancing manner evokes not only the guidance but also the psychic energy needed to carry out the sequence of transformations now required of us as we move into the future.*

The time for such transformations is already upon us. Already millions of people are homeless because of climate change – ten million in Bangladesh alone in recent years. A third of Earth's species are in danger of extinction. Rain forests, coral reefs and fertile topsoil, which are all essential for rich, healthy and sustainable ecosystems, are diminishing throughout the planet every year. Without healthy topsoil, we will not be able to grow enough crops to feed ourselves and have the variety of food that we have become so accustomed to having on our tables. Anodea

Judith also mentions how,

It is not only population growth that must be curbed, but the way we view progress and success. Ever since the Industrial Revolution, progress has been measured by growth. The success of a company is usually defined by its expansion, not its social contribution.

Participating in Nature's progress

A widespread spiritual awareness is needed for humankind to overcome its differences and unite everyone in a common cause for good and a reaffirmation of the rights of all, as well as how to exist in harmony with the diversity of species that have just as much right to live on Earth as we do. If we do not move forward and are not willing to grasp the next stage in human evolvement, life will not be the same as we know it. Great transformations spring from creative and visionary thinking, and when people are motivated enough to adopt and follow through on positive ideas.

Additionally, we could consider one of the most profound questions that can be asked, which was put forward by the scientist Albert Einstein, about whether the universe is a friendly place or not. The amazing conclusion thinkers such as Thomas Berry arrived at, was that it is in fact a friendly place and, indeed, that throughout its history it remarkably seems to have been working for us, instead of against us.

If we consider that there have been numerous times when the universe could have wiped us out, yet it has been more than benevolent and supplied us with favourable conditions to inhabit Earth and flourish, it would appear that cosmic forces are supporting us. But now our current age requires us to participate in furthering Earth's progress, which involves conscious effort and beneficially focused energies if we are to continue to live in such an awe inspiring and wondrous place.

Thomas Berry believed the great work was yet to be done. We stand in a special position, where we have to become involved in the making of a New Earth. All it will take is a switch in direction and a re-evaluation of the things we wish to protect and preserve for future generations to come, to take us into the next stage of spiritual evolution and live harmoniously with all.

CARING FOR OUR
SACRED EARTH

CHAPTER
NINE

*We have been trying to go into the future as a human
community in an exploitative relationship with the natural
community without any sense of being integral with this
natural world as a sacred community. From now on,
that is just not acceptable, purely and simply, because it is
a way, not of life, but of death.*

– THOMAS BERRY

There is obviously a need for us to consider how
to cultivate compassionate and caring qualities of our
nature. There is a global cry for humankind to think about
changes that do not merely favour a chosen few. Part of this
is related to the importance of proactive education, helping
people grasp effective solutions to contemporary problems,
and what we can do to bring about justice, fairness, peace,
equality, sisterhood and brotherhood into our immediate
communities, as well as in the wider world around us.

If we take a leaf from the pages of Nature, which are
about diversity and equilibrium, we can learn how to go
forward. If we follow her example and are maturely sensitive
enough to the differences that make up our human race, and

appreciate how human life is enriched by its different people, beliefs and cultures, we will start to find ways of living peacefully with one another and working together for the good of all. For it will be hard to move on unless it is done together in harmony.

Many contemporary seekers have come a long way from *I am right and you are wrong* prejudices and from seeking to convert people from other faiths and none. Yet the roads leading to and embracing a healthy inclusiveness can be difficult, as it requires stepping out of current modes of thinking and entering unfamiliar territory in order to accept a wider spirituality.

One of the features of psychological and spiritual unfoldment is that inner conflict is often experienced, which can be projected onto others, before new realms of understanding are achieved. A majority of great wisdom traditions teach about stages of growth in which it is sometimes hard to grasp the perspectives of unattained levels of growth until they are reached (the contemporary psychological system Spiral Dynamics also teaches this). This was one reason why the Buddha remained silent on certain points about enlightenment. This inability to understand wider perspectives is why some religious believers are unable to embrace those from other traditions and unite with them in the work that is needed for bringing about a lasting peace in the world and living harmoniously with Nature.

This refusal of accepting others and an authentic compassionate spirituality is found within fundamentalist strands of all traditions. Religions in the hands of narrow thinkers, as we know only too well, can separate people, whereas an all-embracing global and Earth centred spirituality, seeks to unite humanity and include all.

Inclusiveness not only helps us to truly come together with people, but also helps us to find unity with other species, Earth, the universe and the natural world. It is no longer a case of thinking in terms of whether religious and spiritual communities should be getting involved in becoming architects of a new spirituality or not, but about realising that humankind will not be effective enough in bringing about the necessary ecological changes that are called for if we do not. There is an unquestionable need to embrace what it is to be a member of the wider global community. This is not just about individual beliefs and what things we can do; it is also about addressing greater problems of power and materialism. On this subject, a poem by a Swedish child named Tove, sincerely asks the following question:

When the last leaf falls, when the last drop of water dies out, when the ozone layer is already destroyed, will it be too late to understand that money is not going to save us?

Transforming our relationship with Earth

We may believe that social status, the latest gadgets or new items of clothing that make corporate businesses richer will bring us lasting happiness. But the only way to become responsibly human and caring citizens of the world is to simplify our lives, to understand deeper issues of why humans have become addicted to harmful patterns of behaviour and to realise the richness, awe, wonder and variety of life that already exists around us and our interconnected relationship with it.

When the tsunami of 2004 happened, a small village community in Sri Lanka was said to have had few fatalities, even though it was one of the worst hit, because they had not forgotten how to live alongside the natural world and take notice of her signs. They did not know exactly what was going to happen, but they knew enough to move quickly away from the coast and climb high-ground.

Tectonic plate theorists tell us that tsunamis happen because of continents drifting and pressing up against each other. If the tectonic plates did not do this, all Earth's carbon dioxide would evaporate and Earth would become like a frozen sphere. Tectonic plate movement is, therefore, an essential ingredient for life on Earth. As far as scientists can tell, there are no other planets that have this activity. It is what makes Earth so unique, diverse and inhabitable for so many life forms.

If we are to continue living on Earth, we need to not only care for her, but also learn how to read her signs, understand her ways and adapt creatively to living in harmony with her. Earth does not have inexhaustible supplies. "The maternal sea is polluted, the heavens are rent, the forests are being destroyed and the deserts are increasing", Patriach Ignatuis IV of Antioch informs us. Yet there is enough for everyone if we are wise enough and care enough about other people and life we share this incredible planet with. Up to now, the west has invariably either tried to control or plunder the natural resources of our planet, which has often ended in disaster. Continually taking what is not ours to take can only lead to a spiritual poverty of the natural world.

If we truly love Nature, we need to consider how we can help her. We owe our birth to the history of Mother Earth, but now we are threatening the multiplicity of life she has sought to celebrate. It is as though there is a psychological split in our human psyche that on the one hand, realises life would be less rich and joyous if there was not the vast array of trees and wildlife around us and, on the other hand, continues to burn an abundance of fossil fuels, use pesticides, bury harmful waste in the ground and propagate methods of farming that destroy Nature's natural order, balance and biodiversity. In London alone, instead of finding creative solutions, many ancient trees are being pulled up and killed because their roots are damaging buildings.

In contrast to this, an article by Derek Chamberlain and George Polley on Green Spirituality in Japan, described how the Japanese people replanted 400 year old cherry trees that were being threatened by a dam construction project.

Ellen Berstein points out in *The Splendor of Creation* that,

> *... just as we have the power to spoil the creation, we also have the power to make it whole. We have the power to mend the earth and to mend ourselves, to sew the pieces back together again.*
>
> *Mending the earth and our selves demands sustenance and vision. It is a lifelong task. It requires lifelong love.*

Global sisterhood and brotherhood

We often don't act on ecological matters or worry about the sustainability of the natural world, as we often don't immediately see the results of the harm that is being done, or because it is taking place in a distant part of the world and feel it has little to do with us. Sometimes it is because the problems seem too big and unsolvable, so we bury our heads in the sand rather than trouble ourselves thinking about inevitable consequences and what is crying out to be done.

The creativity that is called for requires a responsiveness (which is always needed to help it flourish) that comes from deep within people's hearts, just as when we watch the news and see disaster victims and feel impelled to help. We must realise that people are already suffering because of consumerism and irresponsible farming and manufacturing methods. It is only because the rest of the world has not lived as extravagantly as we have in the west that humanity has not yet reached a point of no return.

A global community working together in the search for finding a deeper and healthier spirituality is one that listens to, and acts upon, universal wisdom that crosses all boundaries and embraces all, and looks for a multiple of ways of implementing it for everyone's benefit (including non-human species). It requires engaging with the world, putting globally friendly practices into action, where *everyone* can be involved and feels valued, and helps people to find lasting and profound meaning and purpose to their existence.

We need a compassion that cares enough for the welfare of all and is prepared to find the skills and abilities needed for overcoming the things that separate us, such as humanity's obsession with power and masculine aggression. Instead of becoming complacent or feeling disempowered, and believing that any form of change in humankind's nature and current direction is impossible, we have to become passionate about what can be done and affirm there is nothing that cannot be achieved when it acted upon with love, and in unity and harmony with the divine's creative energies in the universe.

Peace to the land and all that grows on it.
Peace to the sea and all that swims in it.
Peace to the air and all that flies through it.
Peace to the night and all who sleep in it.
– BLESSING BY RAY SIMPSON

APPENDIX 1

EXERCISES

The following exercises I have used in various workshops with students, who tell me how beneficial they are to do. The meditation exercise is an adaptation of one I put in *The House of Wisdom* (co-authored with Swami Dharmananda). There are of course other books that connect with the creative and Nature centred focus of this book that are primarily exercise manuals, such as Joanna Macy's *Coming Back to Life*, and other works that help us to reconnect with Earth through ritual, prayer and meditation, such as those from Pagan and Wiccan perspectives. Sam Hamilton-Poore's *Earth Gospel* has a superb collection of Christian teachings for reflecting on God's creation.

The list is endless, as creativity and Nature touch our lives in so many ways. We may keep a journal in order to reflect on our unfoldment and our connections with the natural world, meet up with like-minded friends to celebrate major turning points of the year, such as the solstices and equinoxes, practise circle dancing, form local groups that combine a variety of practices, including chanting (the mantra *Om* is said to be the first sound that God created, from which all things were made and is comparable with the opening passage in John's Gospel's: "In the beginning was the Word ...") and sharing our weekly highs and lows, go on walking breaks in areas of great beauty, become more active Green campaigners, develop our creative self through painting, writing poetry and composing music, or simply finding time to just *be* in the tranquillity of the natural world and awaken to its mysteries. The scientist Chris Clarke recommends gazing at a selected creature, plant or tree that we feel drawn to for half an hour and letting it speak to us and see what this practice reveals.

In the following first two exercises you will need a variety of different coloured crayons and some largish sheets of white or coloured paper (around A3 size: 420mm x 297mm). These two exercises help to manifest the creative element in your life, and to recognize and work with and unfold its many dimensions.

The creative self
1. Sit quietly for a few minutes with your eyes closed. Take time to be still and be aware of your body sitting on the chair or cushion you are sitting on and the rhythm of your breath entering in and out of your body. Notice the diaphragm as it rises and falls.

2. Ask yourself, "In what areas of my life am I most creative?"

3. Once you have thought of these areas, choose some coloured crayons that you feel drawn to and free-draw any impressions, images or feelings that come to you. Some

students find writing in various colours is enough and some use a combination of drawings with words. Don't worry if you cannot draw. Those without an artistic eye sometimes display more freedom in their drawing, which can be equally revealing.

4. Put your drawing aside and sit quietly again. This time ask yourself one of the following two questions (depending on which one feels most relevant to you): "Are there any areas of creativity in my life that are blocked?" Alternative question, "What dampens my creative energy and enthusiasm?"

5. Once again, make a mental note of anything that arises and draw or write any impressions, images or feelings. You may find that you want to use different coloured crayons for this question.

6. Put the drawing aside and sit quietly. This time ask yourself, "What is causing this?"

7. Make a mental note of anything that surfaces and draw or write any impressions, images or feelings.

8. Put the drawing aside and sit quietly and now ask yourself, "What do I need to express my creativity more and overcome the appearance of any restrictions?"

9. Make a mental note and draw or write any impressions, images or feelings.

10. Put the drawing aside and sit quietly again and ask yourself, "What form will my creativity take?"

11. Make a mental note of anything that surfaces and draw or write any impressions, images or feelings.

12. Place all drawings in front of you and assess your feelings, thoughts and reflections about each of them. Ask yourself, "What do these drawings reveal to me about my life and creativity and what do I need to do to act on the things revealed?"

The creative will

1. Sit quietly for a few minutes with your eyes closed. Take time to be still and be aware of your body sitting on the chair or cushion you are sitting on and the rhythm of your breath entering in and out of your body. Notice the diaphragm as it rises and falls.

2. Ask yourself, "What does my creative will look like?" In other words, what does your creative energy look like. Creativity is a force within Nature, the cosmos and every one of us and, therefore, has its own energy and impulse. Some writers have written about the wildness of creativity, which we then need to catch hold of and learn how to flow with it through various twisting rapids and streams.

3. Choose some coloured crayons that you feel drawn to and free-draw any impressions, images or feelings that come to you.

4. When you have finished, reflect on your drawing and explore its textures and shades. Ask yourself what it revels to you about the creative divine impulse that is an intrinsic part of who you are.

Prayer

Teach me how to live in balance with all life. Help me to take part in assisting Nature's evolvement and discover mutual beneficial enrichment with our sacred Earth.

Meditation on the interrelatedness of life

The following meditation incorporates the creative use of the imagination and can help to bring the whole of you into balance: body, mind, emotions and Spirit. It takes approximately 25 minutes to practise.

Because of the practice's length, which involves various stages, you may wish to ask a friend to lead you through it or record yourself reading it and meditate to your recording. Be sure to leave an appropriate length of space between each part if you do this. Step 1 is a preliminary settling down stage, which briefly focuses on some elements that are later incorporated as specific stages in the exercise.

1. Relax and breathe normally, slowly and rhythmically, keeping the spine erect. Close your eyes. Become aware of the body. Feel its weight on the chair or cushion you are sitting on. Think about the body and its relation to Earth and the universe, and how it is made of atoms that are the building blocks of all physical life that once made stars,

plants and other life in the universe.

Become aware of the breath as it enters in and out of the body. Realise that every breath you take feeds the plants and in return their oxygen feeds you. Reflect upon your interconnectedness with all life and Nature. Notice if the sun passes behind clouds and makes a difference to the brightness of the place you are sitting in (even with your eyes closed you will notice this).

Listen to any sounds of Nature that can be heard around you – the rustling of leaves in the wind, the singing of birds, the humming or buzzing of insects, the pattering of rain or the trickling of a running stream. Feel the natural vibration of Nature, and feel yourself at one and in harmony with it. Stay with your feelings, thoughts and observations for a while.

2. As you breathe in, mentally say to yourself, 'I breathe in the stabilising Earth element'. As you breathe out, mentally repeat, 'I breathe out the stabilising Earth element'. Repeat this five times.

As you repeat the words, feel Earth's strength entering and connecting with your body – balancing and harmonising all of your body's organs, and making every part of you function optimally, as well as rhythmically with itself and other facets of your being. Feel it healing and grounding the whole of your physical self, bringing strength and vitality. Stay with this element for a while.

3. Become aware of the breath and as you breathe in,

mentally say to yourself, 'I breathe in the soothing water element'. As you breathe out, mentally repeat, 'I breathe out the soothing water element'. Repeat this five times.

As you repeat the words, remember that water is the elixir of all physical life. Feel the soothing effect of the water element gently replenishing you and feel its calming influence. Know that it has the power to restore and refresh your whole being and balance all parts. Stay with this element for a while.

4. Become aware of the breath and as you breathe in, mentally say to yourself, 'I breathe in the rejuvenating sun element'. As you breathe out, mentally repeat, 'I breathe out the rejuvenating sun element'. Repeat this five times.

As you repeat the words, feel the purifying and comforting effects of the sun element transforming you and all inhibiting emotions, feelings and thoughts. Realise that all animal life requires warmth to be truly alive and how this warmth and energy comes ultimately from the sun, which gives life to plants that feed you and other life on Earth. Realise it is helping you to let go of all concerns and be more peacefully present in the eternal now of existence and the radiance of eternal goodness. Stay with this element for a while.

5. Become aware of the breath and as you breathe in, mentally say to yourself, 'I breathe in the cleansing air element'. As you breathe out, mentally say, 'I breathe out the cleansing air element'. Do this five times.

As you repeat the words, feel the cleansing and inspiring effect of the air element. Feel a clearness of the mind and a relaxing of the body and emotions. Know that this element is restoring your mind, body, feelings and emotions to health and equal balance with all existence. Stay with this element for a while.

6. Become aware of the breath and as you breathe in, mentally say to yourself, 'I breathe in creativity' (which has links with both *prana* and *shakti* energy in Yoga). As you breathe out, mentally say, 'I breathe out creativity'. Do this five times.

As you repeat the words, feel your mind, consciousness and whole being expanding. Feel it awakening you to your authentic Self and harmonising all parts. Feel it embracing and enveloping you and lifting your consciousness to a higher level of understanding and existence.

Feel the positive energy of creativity permeating everything within you and around you. Know that within this energy you may find time to rest, restore, replenish and purify your whole being – your body, mind, feelings and emotions. Stay with this experience for a while.

7. Become aware of the breath and as you breathe in, mentally say to yourself, 'I breathe in the loving presence of the infinite Self'. As you breathe out, mentally say, 'I breathe out the loving presence of the infinite Self'. Do this five times. Feel all that is pure and good in life. Feel peace, love, joy, light, beauty and harmony. Know that you are a

pure manifestation of the divine. Awaken to and manifest this divinity within you now, and let it shine through and permeate your whole being. Stay with this experience for a while and strengthen your awareness of it.

8. Slowly become aware of your surroundings and collect your thoughts and embody the experiences you have awakened to in this exercise and take the influence of these experiences into your everyday life.

Affirmation
I am aware of the divine's presence as the unifying creative essence of all. I acknowledge its creativity and compassion as the ground of all existence. I am conscious of my original goodness and of an active, caring, interdependent relationship with every species. I embrace a life of infinite co-creative possibilities with the divine's and the universe's creativity. I am a receptive instrument for truth, love, justice, kindness, harmonious living and wisdom, and awaken to these qualities and actions within my life now.

APPENDIX 2

THE CREATION MYSTICAL JOURNEY

As mentioned in this book, a particular form of creative and creation centred spirituality has been promoted in the last three decades by the Episcopalian and former Dominican priest Matthew Fox, as a key element of both the Christian mystical tradition and many other important mystical and spiritual teachings. It contrasts sharply with mainstream Christian ideas about fall and redemption and instead places strong emphasis on original blessing, in place of original sin.

The term *Creation Centred Spirituality* was first suggested as a name for this creative and mystical branch of spirituality in the late 1960s by Fox's college mentor, the French Theologian, Pere Chenu. GreenSpirit is a UK based version of Creation Spirituality ideals, with members from around the globe. It honours Nature as a great teacher, the interconnected sacredness of all life, affirms differences and the prophetic voice of artists.

Within the Christian mystical tradition, Creation Spirituality traces its roots back to the Old and New Testament and the cosmological wisdom of the early eastern mystics and medieval Christians, such as Hildegard of Bingen, Francis of Assisi, Thomas Aquinas, Meister Eckhart and Julian of Norwich. From non-Christian traditions, it finds common ground with indigenous beliefs and practices, middle and far eastern spiritualities and contemporary science.

It is not looked upon as a new tradition, but one that has been rediscovered in the west. It affirms diversity and seeks wholeness and unity between male and female, homosexual, bisexual and heterosexual, different races and cultures, Christians and non-Christians, Earth, the world of Nature and humans. It has deep connections with the intuitive, creative, caring and compassionate elements of spirituality – qualities of the archetypal anima/feminine or Goddess principle – with liberation theology and justice for the oppressed.

The following is a summary of what Matthew Fox sees as four elements/routes of the Creation Mystical Journey, drawn from his own summary in *Wrestling with the Prophets*:

1. Via Positivia

Experiencing the divine as delight, awe and wonder, which is available to us in every moment. Such experiences can be found in everyday work, Nature, relationships, art, lovemaking, silence and even in times of suffering. It is about seeing the divine in all – the Cosmic Christ in the Christian tradition.

2. Via Negativa

Experiences of darkness, as in the Dark Night of the Soul

and suffering that can be encountered in daily life and on the mystical journey. It encompasses times of letting go and letting be, and profound life changing experiences that can be awakened to when we surrender ourselves and all things to God. Such experiences may happen when sensory experiences are released, as in times of meditation and fasting. It is a time of renewal, new birth and new light, brought about through this path/stage, where we come to realise a deeper mystery within that has no name.

3. Via Creativa

A call to be co-creators with God, which can be achieved through art as meditation, where we trust our creative thoughts and give birth to, as well take responsibility for, them – as creativity can also be destructive as well as beneficial to life, humanity, society and Earth. It is about being known through what we do, and knowing our hidden treasures, gifts and abilities and manifesting them.

4. Via Transformativa

The mystical journey culminates, but never ends, as it is ever-expanding and in a transformation that reveals itself most in the practice of compassion – a prime quality of the Creator. It is also a celebration of our shared interests and a healing by way of justice-making and the realisation of universal laws – that accept unity in diversity – to live by.

Twelve Principles

In *Originally Blessed*, which was edited by Matthew Henry

and published to celebrate the 25th anniversary of Matthew Fox's influential book *Original Blessing*, it outlines Twelve Principles of Creation Spirituality:

1. The Universe, and all within it, is fundamentally a blessing. *Our relationship with the universe fills us with awe.*

2. In Creation, God is both immanent and transcendent. This is panentheism which is not theism (God out there) and not atheism (no God anywhere). *We experience that the divine is in all things and all things are in the divine.*

3. God is as much Mother as Father, as much Child as Parent, as much God in mystery as the God in history, as much beyond all words and images as in all forms and beings. *We are liberated from the need to cling to God in one form or one literal name.*

4. In our lives, it is through the work of spiritual practice that we find our deep and true selves. *Through the arts of meditation and silence we cultivate a clarity of mind and move beyond fear into compassion and community.*

5. Our inner work can be understood as a four-fold journey involving:

- Awe, delight, amazement (*Via Positiva*).
- Uncertainty, darkness, suffering, letting go (*Via Negativa*).

• Birthing, creativity, passion (*Via Creativa*).

• Justice, healing, celebration (*Via Transformativa*).

We weave through these paths like a spiral danced, not a ladder climbed.

6. Every one of us is a mystic. *We can enter the mystical as much through beauty (Via Positiva) as through contemplation and suffering (Via Negativa). We are born full of wonder and can recover it at any age.*

7. Every one of us is an artist. *Whatever the expression of our creativity, it is our prayer and praise (Via Creativa).*

8. Every one of us is a prophet. *Our prophetic work is to interfere with all forms of injustice and that which interrupts authentic life (Via Transformativa).*

9. Diversity is the nature of the universe. *We rejoice in and courageously honour the rich diversity within the Cosmos and expressed among individuals and across multiple cultures, religions and ancestral traditions.*

10. The basic work of God is compassion and we, who are all original blessings and sons and daughters of the Divine, are called to compassion. *We acknowledge our shared interdependence; we rejoice at one another's joys and grieve at one another's sorrows and labour to heal the causes of those sorrows.*

11. There are many wells of faith and knowledge drawing from one underground river of divine wisdom. The practice of honouring, learning and celebrating the wisdom collected from these wells is Deep Ecumenicism. *We respect and embrace the wisdom and oneness that arises from the diverse wells of all the sacred traditions of the world.*

12. Ecological justice is essential for the sustainability of life on Earth. *Ecology is the local expression of cosmology and so we commit to live in light of this value: to pass on the beauty and health of Creation to future generations.*

* * *

Websites for further information and how to get involved:

Creation Spirituality Info
creationspirituality.info

Creation Spirituality Communities
(US based network)
originalblessing.ning.com

Friends of Creation Spirituality
www.matthewfox.org

GreenSpirit
(UK based network and publishers of the GreenSpirit Journal)
www.greenspirit.org.uk

GLOSSARY

Advaita (non-dualism) – the belief in there being ultimately only one Reality behind the many forms of life and matter in the universe (both seen and unseen).

Ahimsa (non-harmfulness) – non-violence in thought, word or deed.

Allah – the Islamic word for God.

Altered states of Consciousness – can refer to a variety of different states of consciousness, from drug induced experiences to deep mystical states of awareness.

Anima – in Carl Jung's psychology, anima is the archetypal image of womanhood, which is present in the unconscious of all men.

Animism – a belief that all things, such as trees, plants, rocks and animals, have souls.

Animus – in Carl Jung's psychology, animus is the archetypal image of the masculine, which is present in the unconscious of all women.

Anthropomorphic – giving things or God/s human qualities.

Archetypes – in Jungian psychology archetypes are seen more as universal mental imprints and images, which can have profound spiritual meanings and a transforming influence on those who have experience of them.

Atman (Self) – the eternal true Self in Hindu spirituality that can be seen as individual, universal and transcendent and connects with the ultimate ground of all (see Brahman).

Attunement – the ability to blend/attune one's awareness with psychic, spiritual or mediumistic states of consciousness. It functions in numerous ways, such as how we relate to Nature, with all life and the many aspects of the divine within us and in all things.

Awareness – the ability to have conscious knowledge of oneself and exterior life, and includes knowledge of various states of spiritual consciousness.

Awe – a sense of mystery, wonder, reverential respect and transcendence that inspires us. It can be awakened within us, when we become aware that we live, move and have our being in a sacredness permeating and transcending all.

Authentic/True Nature or Self – the part of our being that is divine and connects with all. It can be viewed as having an individual, universal and ultimate transcendent facet to it, which has the power to harmonise conflicting parts into a synthesised and sacred whole, and help us to find unity with all. Modern psychology also uses these terms, but will not necessarily relate them with the divine. Branches of Buddhism use the term 'Buddha Nature' instead of authentic or true Self.

Bhakti Yoga (devotion/love) – a devotional path towards the divine or projected onto a teacher as a manifestation of the divine.

Bindu (point) – the chakra or psychic centre that is seen to be associated with the moon and psychic sounds. There is also a cosmic form of *bindu*, which is seen as a source point and centre of energy from which everything was created.

Bodhi (enlightenment) – the state of any enlightened being or Buddha.

Bodhisattva (enlightened being) – in Mahayana Buddhism it is someone who has vowed to put off her or his own final enlightenment in order to help others.

Brahman – in Hindu spirituality it is the one ultimate Reality within and beyond the many forms of the universe.

Buddha (one who is awake) – someone who is enlightened and has woken up to the Truth and is seeing things clearly and as they really are. It also refers to the historical Buddha.

Buddha Nature – there are two aspects to it: developable and naturally abiding within us. It transcends thought, is thoroughly pure, undefiled, empty of all dualities and experienced as a joyous expansiveness with infinite positive potential.

Buddhi – intuitive and discerning faculty, which in its highest form, draws upon the consciousness of the *atman*, or in its lowest, categories of sensory information.

Celtic Spirituality – links with Neo-Paganism, Neo-Druidism and the early medieval Christianity of Britain and Ireland.

Cenozoic Age – our current period in Earth's history.

Chakra (wheel) – a principal energy centre in the psychic/subtle body.

Chi – in Daoism it is the vital and primordial energy and life force, the cosmic spirit that pervades and gives life to all things.

Chit (consciousness) – absolute pure consciousness.

Collective Unconscious – a universal interconnected consciousness acting within the cosmos. Carl Jung believed it housed powerful archetypes and memories that can be traced back to the beginnings of human thought.

Consciousness – to have a level of self-awareness. In spiritual traditions consciousness is not seen to rely on just the physical body for its existence and is often viewed as functioning in numerous ways, such as on an individual and universal level, as well as in ultimate transcendent states of mystical experience.

Contemplation – can simply refer to reflecting on life and one's experiences. In Christian mysticism it is a form of prayer that is comparable to Yogic and Buddhist forms of meditation.

Cosmic Intelligence or Cosmic/Universal Consciousness – a creative interconnected mind that came into being with the Creation of the universe, of which we are all a unique part of, which can be realised in transcendent states of consciousness.

Cosmology – a form of science that looks at the origins and the growth of the universe.

Cosmological Argument – philosophical arguments that look for an infinite chain of causes, which can be traced back to one ultimate cause.

Creation Centred Spirituality – a spirituality which looks for ways to become co-creators with the divine and find harmony with the creative mind of the universe. Its roots can be found in various traditions. It embraces diversity, the findings of contemporary science, ecological issues and justice for the oppressed. The visionary activist Matthew Fox has done much to promote the teachings of Creation Spirituality over the last few decades.

Daoism/Taoism – a strongly Nature based Chinese tradition, which places emphasis on the three jewels of compassion, moderation and humility.

Dark Night of the Soul – a period of spiritual dryness that is seldom lit by any uplifting spiritual experience. Nonetheless, it is invariably seen as a stage of progression on the spiritual path.

Deep Ecology – a term coined by the influential Norwegian philosopher Arne Naess in 1972. It has since become a branch of ecological philosophy and psychology, which emphasizes the equal value of human and non-human life. Its ideas are open to people from different backgrounds and beliefs to use. In 1984, Arne Naess, along with George Sessions, formulated what is called the Deep Ecology Platform, which at it heart, has eight-points for bringing about positive changes in the environment.

Dharma (bearer) – has many meanings, such as law, righteousness, virtue, duty or truth, such as the truth of the Buddha's teachings, which one might have first-hand experience and insight into. In orthodox Hinduism, *dharma* is also associated with one's individual duties (*svadharma*) dependent on one's caste.

Dhikr – a word used by Sufis meaning 'remembrance' and refers to the practice of remembering God often.

Disidentification – the ability to own different parts of ourselves, such as our bodies, feelings and mind, or things that we usually associate our lives with, and realising that we are much more than them.

Divine – an ultimate sacred interconnectedness, which works and is universally present within our cosmos and also transcends it.

Divine Feminine – seeing Earth, Nature and the cosmos as created by and possessing qualities of the divine Mother.

Duhkha (unsatisfactoriness) – one of three marks of existence in Buddhism. It is often translated as 'suffering' into English, but the word 'unsatisfactoriness' is now seen as a more accurate translation.

Ecological Self – a term coined by the influential Norwegian philosopher Arne Naess. It involves transcending restrictive levels of self-interest in order to embrace a wider circle of eco-friendly spirituality.

Ecopsychology – a school of psychology that looks into deeper issues of unhealthy patterns of human behaviour and human relationships with the natural world. The professor of history at California State University, Harvard, Theodore Roszak, is a founder of Ecopsychology and was possibly the first to use the term in his book *The Voice of the Earth*, first published in 1992.

Ecozoic Age – a phase of Earth's history requiring humans to live at one with its needs and finding mutually beneficial enrichment.

Ecumenical – originally a movement within Christian spirituality seeking to unite different Christian denominations, which has since been widened by some to also be about seeking unity amongst different world religions.

Ego – it can have different interpretations. In mystical and eastern wisdom it refers to our individual sense of self, to self-centredness and how we see ourselves as separate from other life.

Enlightenment – a state of being where one has woken-up to seeing and embodying the ultimate truth, although different traditions and branches of faith have various views about it.

Equanimity – a state of calmness, composure and balance.

Earth Charter – adopted in the year 2000 with the aim of addressing economic, social, political and environmental issues facing our current world.

Etheric Energy – comparable with *prana* and *chi* energy, and seen as a vital energy working in and surrounding the body and as a universal life-force.

Ethno-centric – a tribal mentality which only cares about those who share the same interests or beliefs, or people closest to them. A stage between being ego-centric and world-centric.

Existential – relating to existence.

Fana – a word used by Sufis meaning 'passing away', and refers to dying to the world and finding survival in God.

Flow – a state of being where an individual feels at one with all actions and life.

Gaia – a term used for Earth when seen as a living and self-regulating organism.

Global Spirituality – spirituality concerned with global issues.

Global Warming – the rise in the average temperature of Earth's air and oceans, created by fossil burning fuels increasing carbon dioxide in the atmosphere.

Grace – a blessing and/or gift from God that helps a seeker move forward in her or his evolvement. Life and Creation itself are also seen as gifts from God and, therefore, part of God's grace in traditions such as Christianity and Judaism and some devotional schools of Hinduism. Arguably, the concept of grace is not in the historical Buddha's teachings, whereas later in different strands of Mahayana Buddhism a form of grace that helps spiritual seekers is mentioned.

Great Spirit – a term used to describe the Creator in Native American spirituality and other indigenous traditions.

GreenSpirit (UK network of Creation Spirituality) – celebrates all life as deeply interconnected and sacred. It includes the insights of contemporary science, the freedom of creativity, the passion of social action and the wisdom of spiritual traditions.

Guides/Spirit Guides – discarnate spirit personalities that are believed to interact with the physical world and aid people's development.

Guides/Spiritual Guides – people who help others in their spiritual growth, such as a guru in the Yogic tradition.

Gunas (qualities) – three qualities in the Hindu Yogic tradition that are said to interact constantly with each and create a sense of separateness from our authentic nature.

Guru (teacher) – can refer either to a spiritual teacher who dispels darkness or to the divine/God as the Supreme Guru.

Hatha Yoga (yoga of force) – a branch of Yoga that places emphasis on physical postures, cleansing techniques and breathing exercises.

Healer – someone who heals with the interaction of the spirit world, or through the use of prayer or affirmations, or anyone who can restore someone to a state of well-being through a variety of methods, such as naturopathic remedies, holistic practices, acupuncture, or the laying-on of hands at an Evangelical meeting.

Higher Self – a part of us which houses our finest attributes and qualities, such as compassion, kindness and wisdom.

Holiness – a state of being near to God, being holy or made whole.

Holistic – including and harmonising the whole self: the body, feelings, emotions, mind and spiritual levels of being.

'I'/the 'I' – the individual self that we see as separate from other people and things, which has associations with the ego (self-centredness). It should be noted that western psychology has many different theories about the ego.

'I'/the True 'I' Consciousness – the ultimate Self/Reality (a non-separate Reality).

Illumination – mystical visions, experiences and openings of the mind and consciousness.

Immanent – when used to refer to the divine, it refers to the divine as being ever-present.

Integral Spirituality – a spirituality that includes many traditions, disciplines, insights and practices of both the east and west, such as modern science and psychology, and eastern philosophy and practices, and looks for an integration of the spiritual whole of our individual, social and universal selves.

Integral Yoga – a systemised path of self-discovery and expression formulated by Sri Aurobindo: a unitive path of perfection, bhakti (devotion), jnana (insight and knowledge) and karma (action) yoga, which aims for a spiritual purification and transformation of the complete personality.

Interconnectedness (non-separateness) – that everything shares an interrelationship.

Inter-faith – seeking for an open dialogue, and an acceptance of difference and finding of common ground between different faiths.

Interspirituality – a contemporary term coined by the lay monk, Brother Wayne Teasdale, who was a friend of Father Bede Griffiths. It seeks to overcome barriers between different faiths and incorporate practices and insights from various traditions, particularly Hindu and Christian spirituality.

Intuition – the ability to know information without the aid of the physical senses. In spiritual literature intuition is often associated with wisdom and profound levels of insight, but it can function in everyday levels of knowing about something being right or wrong, or everyday hunches.

Jivatman (individual self) – individual 'I' and consciousness, which also has connections with the divine as our innermost being.

Jnana Yoga (yoga of knowledge) – yogic path to freedom via wisdom, discernment and intuitive insight.

Kabbalah – a mystical branch of the Jewish wisdom tradition.

Karma (action) – refers to 'actions having consequences' and the will, which, therefore, have an effect on one's spiritual progress, in either a positive or negative way, in this life or a future one.

Karma Yoga (yoga of action) – a path that leads to spiritual liberation through skilful willed actions.

Kashmir Shaivism – an Indian tradition that believes there is no separation between God and the world.

Kundalini Shakti (coiled energy) – the manifested spiritual power or serpent energy that exists in the individual.

Kundalini Yoga (yoga of psychic energy) – a path that seeks liberation through the use of creative psychic energy.

Liberation – freedom from psychological states and worldly conditioning which restrict the true spiritual nature of our being.

Lower Self – part of our being that is in disharmony with its true spiritual nature.

Mandala (circle) – circular design representing the universe and a particular deity.

Mantra Yoga – the repetition of mantras as a path to liberation. Words, sounds or short affirmations are repeated in order to affirm an aspect of the divine, which is invariably represented by the name of a specific deity. In Mahayana Buddhism mantras are often used for bringing about an awakening to spiritual qualities within oneself and insights into the ultimate nature of existence.

Maya – can have many meanings, such as the ultimate creative Power in the universe or the world of 'illusion' or 'delusion' in Hindu spirituality. It can also be interpreted as 'misconceptions'.

Meditation – can imply many different types of practices. In Christian spirituality meditation can refer to visualisations and more reflective practices. In the Yogic tradition it can be about focusing one's attention on an object, or on the breath or on a mantra. The contemporary Christian Meditation Movement, founded by the English Benedictine monk, John Main, promoted yogic forms of meditation, such as mantra and various breathing exercises.

Mediumship – the ability to see, hear or feel spirit personalities that no longer have a physical existence. Additionally, trance and physical mediumship and healers who are aided by spirit personalities are other areas that fall under this heading. The word literally refers to someone who is in the middle of two realms of existence and acts as a mediator between the two.

Metaphysics – a form of philosophy dealing with laws that transcend physical laws, and with levels of being, knowing and first cause principles, such as the ultimate cause of creation.

Mind/Higher Mind – a wide term, which has connections with the discriminating faculty and the rational mind (the intellect), as well as wisdom and insight.

Mind/Lower Mind – automatic functions of the mind and sensory perceptions.

Mind/Unconscious Mind (individual unconscious) – levels of the mind that we are not consciously aware of, which include instinctual drives and memories of all past experiences that can affect our personality. The spiritual, psychic and psychological implications of an unconscious mind are vast, as it cannot only be seen to link with parts of ourselves that carry subliminal influences that affect our conduct, but also with the collective unconscious mind that links with all things in the universe.

Mindfulness Meditation – generally refers to a form of Buddhist meditation, that especially focuses on the in- and out-flow of the breath.

Moksha (liberation) – freedom from conditioned worldly existence.

Monism – the belief in there being ultimately only one Reality behind the many forms of life and matter in the universe (both seen and unseen).

Morphogenetic Fields – a biological field permeating Nature, which contains information to shape the exact form of living things, as well as its behaviour. Cambridge biologist Rupert Sheldrake is particularly known for this theory, and has comparisons with Carl Jung's theory of the Collective Unconscious. It has many psychic and spiritual implications concerning an interconnected creative and psychic mind working within Nature.

Mystic – a person who seeks through meditation or contemplative prayer to attain unity with the divine.

Mystical Experience – a wide variety of experiences are often placed under this heading, but a true mystical experience would imply having an experience of union or oneness with the divine.

Mysticism – sometimes seen as almost impossible to define, but can be about a life of prayer and/or meditation, work and discipline dedicated to serving and finding unity with the divine.

Myths – myths or legends about heroic struggles or personal sacrifice can be seen as powerful archetypes – as symbolic metaphors for the spiritual journey. Joseph Campbell found many myths that were common to all wisdom traditions, which tell important stories about the spiritual seeker's individual search for Truth and her or his return home.

Nature Mysticism – spiritual experiences and practices that are connected with Nature.

Neo-Paganism/Wicca – Neo-Paganism covers a range of beliefs, practices and rituals that have emerged and have been rediscovered in recent decades, including Wicca. On the whole, Neo-Paganism is not text based, and seeks to find ways of living in harmony with the world of Nature and places emphasis on the divine feminine.

Nirvana – a state of enlightenment achieved primarily through meditation practices.

Niyama (restraint) – the second limb of Patanjali's Yoga Sutra consisting of five inner observances.

Non-attachment – it is essential to understand that non-attachment is not about being aloof and separate from life. Just as we would not consider the cure of an illness as being about taking medicine that merely numbs our feelings and physical senses and makes us unaware of any pain. Non-attachment encompasses acknowledgment of and being unbound by any restrictive feeling or mental state.

Non-dualism (non-separateness) – the belief that while all things appear to have an individual uniqueness, everything interconnects with an underlying unity (see Monism).

Observer, the – a non-attached observer consciousness, which is usually called the 'witness consciousness' in Yoga and should not be confused with an aloofness.

Om/Aum – the sacred sound from which the universe was created, which symbolizes the ultimate Reality. It is the highest name of the divine. The repetition of *Om* is said to be a potent sound for awakening to one's spiritual consciousness. It is used in both Tibetan Buddhism and in Hindu Yoga.

Omnipotent – all-powerful.

Omnipresence – everywhere and in everything.

Omniscient – all-knowing.

Oneness – a state of being in harmony with all things.

Pantheism – the belief in a divinity that is present in all things.

Panentheism – the belief in a divinity that is present in all things in the universe and beyond. An omnipresent and transcendent divinity.

Perennial Wisdom – a belief that underlying all the great wisdom traditions there is a universal truth running through them.

Pluralism – theologically implies there being more than one principle at work in the universe.

Prana – in the Yogic tradition it is the vital energy in the body and is a universal life-force.

Pranayama – the practice of overcoming limitations of the body and mind through the use of *pranic*/psychic energy, particularly with the aid of breathing exercises.

Prayer – there are many forms of prayer. For example, some Christian practices of contemplative prayer are comparable to eastern practices of meditation. Other forms of prayer can include affirmations, reflecting on sacred texts or asking for divine help.

Projection – negative parts of our character that are denied and projected onto others.

Psyche – the inner instrument through which we think, feel and discriminate. It consists of the lower, higher and unconscious mind and the individual sense of self.

Psychic – someone who has the ability to know things without the aid of the physical senses, or something that cannot be explained by accepted laws of science. The word also refers to psychological levels of being and levels connected with the unconscious mind.

Psychic Abilities – different traditions call psychic abilities by different names, such as the *siddhis* in Hindu Yoga, in which the ultimate siddhi is the realisation of one's true nature and liberation from restrictive states of existence.

Psychosynthesis – a school of transpersonal psychology founded by the Italian psychologist Roberto Assagioli.

Quantum Theory – an area of science that studies the laws of physics that are happening on a very small scale. Of particular interest in this field is the discovery that on a sub-atomic level there is no clear separation between people, objects and other phenomena – that there is an ultimate interconnectedness between all.

Quran – the holy book of the Islamic tradition.

Reincarnation – the belief that after-death the soul is reborn into another physical body, or into another realm, such as the heavenly realm, or the realm of hungry ghosts or fighting demons, as mentioned in the Buddhist tradition. But it should be noted that these realms can also be interpreted as different psychological states of being that we slip in and out of numerous times a day.

Sacred – that which embodies the truth of a religion or an aspect of divinity and is, therefore, something to be in awe of, as well as revered, respected and cherished because of its preciousness.

Saint – another word for a holy person; someone who is seen as virtuous and lives or lived in the divine's presence.

Samadhi – the climax of Yogic meditation practices where one realises the true Self.

Samsara – the world of conditioned existence in the physical world, which is tied-up with ideas about the continual cycle of lives: birth, death and rebirth. It is seen as a world of unsatisfactoriness that we reinforce individually and collectively with our minds and beliefs, which do not show us how things really are.

Samskara – unconscious imprints and impressions left by volitionary acts, which affect our psychological self (see karma)

Satyagraha – a philosophy and practice of nonviolent resistance developed by Mohatma Gandhi, which influenced people such as Martin Luther King jr. in his campaign for racial equality.

Seer – someone who has visions of a prophetic nature and/or can perceive things beyond physical realms of existence.

Self-actualisation – a term used by the American psychologist Abraham Maslow to describe a level of personal development where an individual is able to draw upon and use to their full abilities and potential. Someone who is self-actualised is not static, but forever moving forward with her or his realised potential and creativity and finds joyful pleasure in manifesting her or his abilities.

Self-awareness – to be conscious of one's inner feelings, thoughts, emotions, desires, motives, exterior actions and one's True Self.

Self-realisation – to realise one's full potential and/or one's relationship with the divine.

Shadow/the Shadow – the parts of ourselves that we do not accept and are often hard for us to own.

Shakti (power/force) – the ultimate Reality in its creative and female aspect in Hindu spirituality, which acts in the universe. It is also connected with kundalini yoga.

Shaman – someone who has the ability to contact and actively engage with the spirit world.

Shiva (the kindly one) – one of the oldest of the Hindu deities that many have speculated to be depicted on ancient seals found in the Indus Valley area (dating back to 2500 BCE). He is represented as the *lingam*, has three aspects – creative, preserving and destroying – and seen performing the cosmic dance in the form of Shiva-Nataraja in many statues. He has served yogins and yoginis throughout the ages and is sometimes placed as part of the *trimurti*, along with Vishnu and Brahma, as the destroyer.

Shomrei Adamah (Keepers of Earth) – a Jewish environmental organisation started by Ellen Bernstien in the United States of America.

Skilfulness – the ability to be spiritually creative in everyday life and conduct ourselves in a manner that brings about balanced living.

Socially Engaged Spirituality – a spirituality that seeks to bring about beneficial changes in society and the world.

Soul – a wide term that can mean different things to different people. For some it is looked upon as the same as the individual spark of the spirit in all; for others, it can be associated more with the psychological self.

Spiral Dynamics – a bio-psychological system/science that reveals the hidden codes that shape human behaviour. Founded by Clare W. Graves and expanded upon by his associates Don Edwards and Christopher C. Cowan.

Spirit – can have many different meanings, such as one's individual spirit, or used as a plural to refer those who no longer have a physical existence. It can also be used as another word for the divine and the sacredness of all.

Spiritual Emergency – sudden spiritual openings or awakenings that interfere with a spiritual seeker's ability to function properly in her or his daily life. If properly handled, with the support of a reliable and understanding network of friends, community and/or therapist, these experiences can invariably lead to a more healthy state of spiritual growth. The Czechoslovakia psychologist Stanislav Grof and his wife Christina have been particularly influential in bringing this area of spiritual crisis to the attention of various transpersonal psychologists and the public at large through books such as the classic of personal development, *The Stormy Search for the Self.*

Spirit World – can refer to an interconnected reality that permeates all, a spiritual existence, or a world that is inhabited by individual spirit personalities.

Sub-conscious – sometimes used as an alternative word for the unconscious mind, or to describe thoughts, feelings and actions that are just beneath surface levels of awareness, which can be accessed by the conscious mind – termed the 'preconscious' by Sigmund Freud.

Sub-personalities – refers to the many different roles and facets of our personality, such as the parent, the lover, the party-animal and so on.

Subtle Body – a psychic body mentioned in different traditions that can include the *chakras* and different elements (earth, fire, water, air and ether) and energies, as well as emotional and mental realms.

Sufism – a mystical branch of Islam.

Superconsciousness – has associations with different states, such as hearing astral sounds, seeing visions and experiencing cosmic energy, which can lead to a realisation of the divine's omnipresent and transcendent nature. Such things can be seen as being higher and lower levels of superconsciousness, which can lead to an opening to one's authentic spiritual nature.

Surrender (letting go and letting God) – the practice of letting go of the individual will and handing one's thoughts, ideas and actions over to the divine or to more spiritual states of consciousness.

Synchronicity – random events that take on symbolic meaning, such as a bird flying into a room signifying bad news, or natural coincidental events that are seen as miraculous happenings.

Tantra (continuity) – refers to practices and teachings that focus on the use of *shakti* energy.

Teleological Argument – a philosophical argument which looks for proof of God's existence in the design, order and purpose of the world.

Theism – the belief in God or in gods, especially in a Creator God that acts in the universe.

Theology – the study of the nature of, and belief about, God.

Torah – a wide term that includes God's law as revealed to Moses.

Transcendent – levels beyond normal physical experience.

Transpersonal – states of consciousness beyond the boundaries of personal identity.

Transpersonal Psychology – a form of western psychology that includes spiritual and eastern insights and practices, such as the Psychosynthesis school of psychology, founded by Roberto Assagioli.

Unconscious – see 'Collective Unconscious' and 'Mind: Unconscious Mind'.

Unfoldment – a similar word to development, which refers more to the removal of things that stop us from recognizing and manifesting our true spiritual nature. Unfolding authentic qualities and wisdom and working towards a spiritual synthesis that influences the whole of our lives.

Unitive Consciousness – in Christian mysticism it is where the ultimate mystery is realised and the seeker recognizes her or his co-relationship with the Creator. A non-separate consciousness.

Upanishads (sitting down near) – part of the revealed *Vedic* teachings. Primarily mystical teachings that speak from experience of higher states of consciousness, the earliest of which dates back to around 800 BCE.

Vedanta (end of the Vedas) – one of the six classical systems of Hindu philosophy, focusing primarily on the teachings of the *Upanishads, Brahma Sutra* and the *Gita*.

Vishnu – one of the main gods in Hindu spirituality, who is sometimes described as the preserver. The divine figure Krishna is one of his most popular incarnations.

Visionary – in spiritual traditions it can refer to someone who has prophetic gifts or teaches profound wisdom about the future.

Wholism – including and working on the spiritual whole of our existence; from the body, mind and emotions, and the realms of individual, social and global spirituality, to Cosmological spirituality.

Witness Consciousness – can have wide connotations in Yogic literature. From one perspective it links with the practice of mindfulness, a state of pure presence or bare awareness. Here it can be seen as a non-attached impersonal observer consciousness that is separate from the thinking mind. From its highest viewpoint, it can refer to an essence of our divine nature, which transcends seer and seen reality (witnesser and witnessed). The two perspectives are generally not seen as separate from one another, but as one Reality functioning in different ways.

World/Earth-centric – concerned with global issues.

Yahweh – Hebrew word for God.

Yama (discipline) – the first stage of Patanjali's Eight-limbed Yoga dealing with moral and ethical conduct.

Yoga (to yoke/to bind and make whole) – the most popular forms are bhakti, karma and jnana in Hinduism. Yoga is also practised in the Buddhist and Jain traditions.

Yoga Sutra (yogic aphorisms) – a compilation of yogic teachings credited to Patanjali around the 2nd century CE. Also known as *Raja Yoga* (Royal Yoga) and *Classical Yoga*: one of the six classical systems of Hindu philosophy.

Zen – A form of Japanese Buddhism that originally came from China (known as Chan in China, Son in Korea and Thien in Vietnam).

BIBLIOGRAPHY

Ajitsing, Charanjit K. (compiled by), *Wisdom of Sikhism*, Oneworld, Oxford, 2001.

Atlee, Tom, *Reflections on Evolutionary Activism: Essays, Poems and Prayers from an Emerging Field of Sacred Social Change*, Evolutionary Action Press, Eugene, 2009.

Aurobindo, Sri, *A Conception of Supermind in the Veda*, article in *All India Magazine*, Aurobindo Society, Pondicherry, February 2004.

— , *Glossary of Terms in Sri Aurobindo's Writings*, Sri Aurobindo Ashram, Pondicherry, 1978.

— , *The Life Divine*, Sri Aurobindo Ashram, Pondicherry, Reduced Facsimile Edition, 1986.

Beck, Don Edward, and Christopher C. Cowan, *Spiral Dynamics: Mastering Values, Leadership and Change*, Blackwell, Oxford, 1996.

Bernstein, Ellen, *Creation Theology: A Jewish Perspective*, in *The Green Bible: New Revised Standard Version* (with a foreword by Desmond Tutu), HarperOne, New York, 2008.

— , *The Splendor of Creation, A Biblical Ecology*, Cleveland, The Pilgrim Press, 2005.

Berry, Thomas, *The Dream of the Earth*, Sierra Book Club, San Francisco, 1990.

— , *Evening Thoughts: Reflecting on Earth as Sacred Community* (edited by Mary Evelyn Tucker), Sierra Book Club, San Francisco, 2006.

— , *The Great Work: Our Way into the Future*, Bell Tower, New York, 1999.

— , with Thomas Clark, *Befriending the Earth: A Theology of Reconciliation Between Humans and the Earth*, Twenty-third Publications, Mystic, Connecticut, 1991.

Chamberlain, Derek, and George Polley, *Being Green in Japan*, article in *GreenSpirit Journal, Volume 12.1*, GreenSpirit, London, Spring, 2010.

Chopra, Deepak, *Power, Freedom and Grace: Living from the Source of Lasting Happiness*, Amber-Allen Publishing, San Rafael, California, 2006.

Cook, John, *The Book of Positive Quotations*, Fairview Press, Minneapolis, 1993.

Corcoran, Peter Blaze, and A. James Wohlpart (edited by), *A Voice for the Earth: American Writers Respond to the Earth Charter* (with forewords by Homero Aridjis and Terry Tempest Williams), University of Georgia Press, Athens and London, 2008.

Cowell, Sion, *The Teilhard Lexicon: Understanding the Language, Terminology and Vision of the Writings of Pierre Teilhard de Chardin*, Sussex Academic Press, Brighton, 2001.

Dharmananda, Swami, and Santoshan, *The House of Wisdom: Yoga Spirituality of the East and West*, O Books, Winchester and New York, 2007.

Eckhart, Meister, *Meditations with Meister Eckhart* (introduction and versions by Matthew Fox), Bear and Company, Rochester, Vermont, 1983.

Fox, Matthew, *Confessions: The Making of a Post-Denominational Priest*, HarperCollins, New York, 1996.

— , *Creativity: Where the Divine and the Human Meet*, Tarcher/Putnam, 2002.

— , *One River, Many Wells: Wisdom Springing from Global Faiths*, Gateway, Dublin, 2001.

— , *Original Blessing: A Primer in Creation Spirituality*, Tarcher/Putnam, New York, 2000 (reprint).

— , *Wrestling with the Prophets: Essays on Creation Spirituality and Everyday Life*, Tarcher/Putnam, New York, 1995.

— , and Rupert Sheldrake, *Natural Grace: Dialogues on Creation, Darkness, and the Soul in Spirituality and Science*, Doubleday, New York, 1996.

Frawley, David, *Yoga and the Sacred Fire: Self-Realization and Planetary Transformation*, Motilal Barnarsidass, Delhi, 2001.

Hamilton-Poore, Sam, *Earth Gospel: A Guide to Prayer for God's Creation*, Upper Room Books, Nashville, 2008.

Hanh, Thich Nhat, *The Heart of the Buddha's Teachings: Transforming Suffering into Peace, Joy and Liberation*, Parallax Press, Berkley (California), 1998.

Harris, Paul (edited by), *The Fire of Silence and Stillness: An Anthology of Quotations for the Spiritual Journey*, Templegate, Springfield, Illinois, 1995.

Henry, Matthew (edited by), *Originally Blessed: The 25th Anniversary of Matthew Fox's Original Blessing*, Creation Spirituality Communities, Golden Colorado, 2008.

The Holy Bible: Today's New International Version, Hodder and Stoughton,

London, Sydney and Auckland, 2006 (reprint).

Gottlieb, Roger S., *The Oxford Handbook of Religion and Ecology*, Oxford University Press, New York, 2006.

Judith, Anodea, *Waking the Global Heart: Humanity's Rite of Passage from the Love of Power to the Power of Love*, Elite Books, Santa Rosa, 2006.

King, Ursula, *Spirit of Fire: The Life and Vision of Teilhard de Chardin*, Orbis Books, New York, 1996 (5th reprint).

Kumar, Satish, *Spiritual Compass: The Three Qualities of Life*, Green Books, Totnes, Devon, 2007.

Lerner, Michael, *Spirit Matters*, Walsch Books, Boston, 2000.

Main, John, *The Heart of Creation: Meditation – a Way of Setting God Free in the World* (edited by Laurence Freeman), Canterbury Press, Norwich, 2007.

McIntosh, Steve, *Integral Consciousness and the Future Evolution: How the Integral Worldview is Transforming Politics, Culture and Spirituality*, Paragon House, St Paul, Minnesota, 2007.

Meyer, Marvin (translated with an introduction by), *The Gospel of Thomas: The Hidden Saying of Jesus* (with an interpretation by Harold Bloom), HarperSanFrancisco, New York, 1992.

Nasr, Seyyed Hossein, *The Garden of Truth: The Vision and Promise of Sufism, Islam's Mystical Tradition*, HarperOne, New York, 2007.

Parthasarathy, A., *The Eternities: Vedanta Treatise*, A. Parthasarathy, Mumbai, 2007 (14th edition).

Poole, Michael, *User's Guide to Science and Belief*, A Lion Book, Oxford, 2007 (3rd edition).

Primack, Joel, and Nancy Ellen Abrams, *The View from the Centre of the Universe: Discovering our Extraordinary Place in the Cosmos*, Fourth Estate, London, 2006.

Ramdas, Swami, *The Essential Ramdas* (compiled with an introduction by Susunaga Weeraperuma), World Wisdom, Bloomington, Indiana, 2005.

Prime, Ranchor, *Vedic Ecology: Practical Wisdom for Surviving the 21st Century* (includes interviews with Vandana Shiva), Mandala Publishing, Novato CA, 2002.

Sacks, Jonathan, *The Dignity of Difference: How to Avoid the Clash of Civilizations*, Continuum, London and New York, 2007 (revised and reprinted edition).

Santoshan, *Realms of Wondrous Gifts: Psychic, Mediumistic and Miraculous Powers in the Great Wisdom Traditions* (with conversations with Glyn

Edwards), The Gordon Higginson Fellowship, Aylesbury, Buckinghamshire, 2008.

Sarkar, Mahendra Nath, *Hindu Mysticism: Studies in Vaisnavism and Tantricism – Volume 1*, Cosmo Publications, New Delhi, 2003 (reprint).

Schumacher, E. F., *Small is Beautiful,* Harper & Row, New York, 1973.

Sleeth, J. Matthew (edited by), *Teachings on Creation through the Ages*, in *The Green Bible: New Revised Standard Version* (with a foreword by Desmond Tutu), HarperOne, New York, 2008.

Swimme, Brian, and Thomas Berry, *The Universe Story: From the First Primordial Flaring Forth to the Ecozoic Era – A Celebration of the Universe,* HarperCollins, New York, 1992.

Taylor, Bron (edited by), *Encyclopedia of Religion and Nature – Volumes 1 and 2*, Continuum, London, 2008 (reprint).

Teasdale, Wayne, *The Mystic Heart: Discovering a Universal Spirituality in the World's Religions* (with a foreword by his holiness the Dalai Lama), NewWorld Library, California, 1999.

— , *The Mystic Hour: A Day Book of Interspiritual Wisdom and Devotion*, New World Library, Novato, California, 2004.

Teilhard de Chardin, Pierre, *The Human Phenomenon* (translated by Sara Appleton-Weber), Sussex Academy Press, Brighton and Portland, 2003.

Visser, Frank, *Ken Wilber: Thought as Passion,* State University of New York Press, Albany, 2003.

Water, Mark (compiled by), *The New Encyclopedia of Christian Quotations*, John Hunt Publishing, Alresford, Hampshire, 2000 (reprint).

Welwood, John, *Towards a Psychology of Awakening: Buddhism, Psychotherapy, and the Path of Personal and Spiritual Transformation*, Shambala, Boston and London, 2000.

Wilson, Edward O., *The Creation: An Appeal to Save Life on Earth*, W.W. Norton and Company, New York and London, 2006.

DVD reference

Freeman, Fr. Laurence (talk by), *John Main: A Celebration of his Life and Teaching*, Conference at Swanwick, UK, 2007.

Internet references (October 2009)

http://en.wikipedia.org/wiki/Ecological_self
http://theoblogical.org/dlature/itseminary/creaspir/whatis1.html

ABOUT THE AUTHOR

Stephen Wollaston has a deep integral and universal approach to spirituality and is a member of GreenSpirit, their editorial and publishing team, and the designer of the GreenSpirit Journal. He was given the name Santoshan (contentment) by Swami Dharmananda Saraswati Maharaj, and has a creative background as a spiritual writer, graphic designer, artist and musician.

He was the bassist of the New Wave and Punk band The Wasps and is the author of several books on spiritual matters, including *The House of Wisdom, Yoga Spirituality of the East and West* (co-authored with Swami Dhamananda). He holds a degree in religious studies and a post graduate certificate in religious education from King's College London and studied psychosynthesis psychology. He also helped to establish The Gordon Higginson Fellowship with the medium and teacher Glyn Edwards. He prefers to have no labels, unless it be integral non-dualist or creation centred universalist.

The House of Wisdom
Yoga Spirituality of the East and West
Swami Dharmananda and
Santoshan

An essential book for wiseful living today. *The House of Wisdom* draws on a variety of profound insights and numerous important teachings from many of the world's great wisdom traditions.

Sections on Yogic spirituality outline the benefits of mantra, paths to the sacred, understanding interactive dimensions of the true Self and the classic Eightfold Path of Yoga. Various practical meditations and beneficial relaxation practices for discovering and harmonising the spiritual whole of ourselves are also included.

Swami Dharmananda Saraswati Maharaj is the spiritual director of the Dharma Centre for Yoga, Spiritual Awareness and Healing.

Santoshan (Stephen Wollaston) is an insightful spiritual writer and teacher of integral growth.

Published by O Books
ISBN 978-1-846940-24-8
223 pages

'An excellent book. *The House of Wisdom* is a real treasure-house of spiritual knowledge.'
– Julie Friedeberger, author of *The Healing Power of Yoga.*

GreenSpirit
Path to a New Consciousness
Edited by Marian Van Eyk McCain

Only by understanding the Universe as a vast, holistic system and Earth as a unit within it can we help restore balance to that unit.

Only by placing Earth and its ecosystems – about which we now understand so much – at the centre of all our thinking can we avert ecological disaster.

Only by bringing our thinking back into balance with feeling, intuition and awareness and by grounding ourselves in a sense of the sacred in all things can we achieve a new level of consciousness.

Green spirituality is the key to a new, twenty-first century consciousness. And here is the most comprehensive book ever written on green spirituality.

Published by O Books
ISBN 978-1-84694-290-7
282pages

'GreenSpirit: Path to a New Consciousness offers numerous healing and inspiring insights; notably, that Earth and the universe are primary divine Revelation, a truth to be transmitted to our children as early and effectively as possible.'
– Thomas Berry.

BOOKS

O is a symbol of the world, of oneness and unity. In different cultures it also means the "eye," symbolizing knowledge and insight. We aim to publish books that are accessible, constructive and that challenge accepted opinion, both that of academia and the "moral majority."

Our books are available in all good English language bookstores worldwide. If you don't see the book on the shelves ask the bookstore to order it for you, quoting the ISBN number and title. Alternatively you can order online (all major online retail sites carry our titles) or contact the distributor in the relevant country, listed on the copyright page.

See our website www.o-books.net for a full list of over 500 titles, growing by 100 a year.

And tune in to myspiritradio.com for our book review radio show, hosted by June-Elleni Laine, where you can listen to the authors discussing their books.

mySpiritRadio